PHILADELPHIA PHENOMS

The Most Amazing Athletes to Play in the City of Brotherly Love

Michael Baumann

SPORTS
PUBLISHING

Sports Publishing books may be purchased in bulk at special discounts for sales promotion, corporate gifts, fund-raising, or educational purposes. Special editions can also be created to specifications. For details, contact the Special Sales Department, Sports Publishing, 307 West 36th Street, 11th Floor, New York, NY 10018 or sportspubbooks@skyhorsepublishing.com.

Sports Publishing® is a registered trademark of Skyhorse Publishing, Inc.®, a Delaware corporation.

Visit our website at www.sportspubbooks.com.

10 9 8 7 6 5 4 3 2 1

Library of Congress Cataloging-in-Publication Data is available on file.

Cover design by Richard Rossiter
Cover photo credit AP Images

Print ISBN: 978-1-61321-711-5
Ebook ISBN: 978-1-61321-737-5

Printed in the United States of America

CONTENTS

CONTENTS

INTRODUCTION

I'm not the kind of person who usually gets to write books like this one. I own several books like this one—books that chronicle Philadelphia sports history through the lens of lists and debates, and they usually get written by a particular kind of person: a veteran of local media, a sort of living, breathing institutional memory, with a personal investment in a particular philosophy of sports: that sports culture in Philadelphia is unique, and that the attitudes of its fans and the norms and values those fans cherish demand a particular kind of athlete.

We define ourselves this way, I believe, in opposition to our more celebrated rivals in New York, Boston, Washington, Atlanta, and Dallas, among other places. It's a natural reaction not only to the unending cultural beatdown the Delaware Valley in general—and Philadelphia in particular—takes as the unclean caste of the Northeast Corridor. While we may see this as a false personification of the City of Brotherly Love, nobody else does, since so much of our country's media and culture comes from Boston, Washington, and New York. It's easy to develop an inferiority complex in the face of such relentless cultural abuse.

And as if by design, our sports teams have been atypically unsuccessful. Either they come heartbreakingly close to winning, then stumble at the finish line, or they dredge the bottom of the standings like a flounder hiding from a predator. So if we're not going to be better, we have to be different, somehow distinct or even righteous to make up for the lack of tangible success. That's how the story goes, anyway, and that's the myth we often buy into.

I don't know that I do, though. I'm a lifelong and unapologetic five-sport Philadelphia fan, imbued with the overriding anger and pessimism that stifles the air around Broad and Pattison like a radioactive haze, but I'm not the typical Philadelphia sports fan, and I can't write like I am. I'm from South Jersey, the oldest son of two non-Philadelphians who didn't pay attention to sports until I developed an obsession with the 1993 Phillies. We didn't go to many games or tailgate—in fact, I saw both the Eagles and Sixers live for the first time as a credentialed member of the media. I was largely a self-taught sports fan, and I learned through books and broadcasts.

I'm not a typical Philadelphia sports fan because I prefer baseball and hockey to football (and nowadays, college football to the NFL) and the NBA to college basketball. I like soccer. I don't think the referees and the national media are out to get us, and I find our collective inferiority complex and affinity for violence to be embarrassing sometimes. I tend to take a long-term outlook on team success and believe that a team's problems are often created—and are past the point of being solvable—years before they manifest themselves.

The other reason I'm not the kind of person who usually gets to write books like this is that greatness is a subjective concept, and subjective debates tend to have less to do with facts or history than they do about the participants' intractable biases and beliefs. Greatness is a nebulous concept that most people redefine to the definition that most conveniently fits their chosen candidate for greatness. Even when defined in good faith, greatness means different things to different people, and the same is true of greatness seen in athletes. If you asked 10 knowledgeable fans to list the 20 greatest athletes in Philadelphia sports history, I doubt that all 10 lists would have more than a handful of names in common. For transparency's sake, here's how I chose mine.

First, I restricted my list to professional team sport athletes who played most of their professional careers in Philadelphia. Measuring baseball players from the 1950s against football players from the 2000s is hard enough without having to parse whether Joe Frazier, a South Carolinian who trained in Philadelphia as a pro, is more of a Philadelphian than Carl Lewis, a South Jerseyan who trained in California. It eliminates greater athletes than the ones listed here who only made a pit stop in Philadelphia professionally: Joe Morgan, Chris Pronger, Pedro Martinez, and so on. It eliminates athletes like Dawn Staley, accomplished athletes who exist in the culture as Philadelphians, but spent the majority of their professional careers elsewhere.

I tried to judge each player based on his on-field accomplishments as a professional in Philadelphia primarily, without ignoring the context in which it occurred. So Tom Gola and Chuck Bednarik get credit for what they did at La Salle and Penn, respectively, while Wilt Chamberlain gets credit for his accomplishments as a Los Angeles Laker (as if he needs the help). I acknowledge Richie Ashburn's career as a broadcaster, Gola's career in local politics, and Bobby Clarke's career as an executive as well.

But while anecdotes and off-the-field popularity flesh out an athlete's public image, they're not what makes him (or her) great. To judge a player's on-field accomplishments, the primary source of truth I looked at is the statistical record, if it exists. As we all know, reputation can be distorted over time.

Where I could, I found statistics that adjusted for level of competition and style of play. Failing that, I tried, as best I could, to factor that in on my own. I leaned heavily on where these players ranked relative to their teammates and relative to the league rather than relying blindly on raw numbers. I also tried to use the statistics that gave me the most accurate picture of the player's performance, particularly in baseball, where advanced historical statistics are most readily available and I understand them best.[1]

You might also notice that this list skews to more recent players. This is intentional: the quality of play across sports has never been higher than it is now. Not only are athletes

---

1 Whenever I mention wins above replacement (WAR), I used the Baseball Reference variety unless stated otherwise.

bigger, stronger, and faster, but also the best athletes have a higher probability of being funneled into professional sports, thanks to globalization, advancements in scouting, and player development and financial incentives.

Baseball, for instance, only became baseball as we know it fairly recently—when Richie Ashburn signed his first professional contract in 1945, Major League Baseball comprised 16 teams, none farther west than St. Louis, populated entirely by white Americans. There was no draft, no divisional play, and only the beginnings of an organized farm system. Most players worked offseason jobs and standards of professionalism and fitness were laughable by today's standards.

Today, MLB features players from around the world, many of whom have trained unceasingly since early childhood for the sole purpose of playing professional baseball. I believe that if you had a time machine and dropped 2007 Chase Utley into the National League in 1950, he'd hit about .700. If you took someone as big and strong as 1995 Eric Lindros into the NHL of 1974, when there were no European players, no composite sticks, and no butterfly goalies, he'd score 150 goals a year.

With that said, recognizing the advancement of quality of play shouldn't mean punishing Chamberlain or Clarke for having been born so early, so I tried to strike a balance.

One final note: you might notice that this list includes a relatively even distribution of athletes according to sport: five each from baseball, hockey, and basketball; four from football, and one from soccer. This is also intentional.

My primary goal was to find 20 great Philadelphia athletes. My secondary goal was to use those athletes' careers to tell significant stories in Philadelphia sports history, from what actually made the Broad Street Bullies so great, to the history of the Warriors—the NBA team that came before the Sixers— to the rise of soccer fanaticism in the past decade. Most of the time, this happened organically, as great athletes tend to be the cause of great sports stories. But I'd be lying if I didn't admit to massaging the rankings somewhat to make sure certain parts of history were represented.

Philadelphia sports culture so often confines us to one way of looking at things. I wanted to acknowledge our history while looking at it from a new perspective and examining what, if anything, makes our culture special. While I certainly reach conclusions in the coming chapters, I'm less interested in the end result than in how we got there.

This list is the result of my own personal philosophy and beliefs, as well as those principles. I don't consider it to be absolute or definitive. (In fact, later on I'll get to how this list might change in the coming years.)

So if you disagree, feel free to make your own list. This list is the product of how I read history and how I judge players— it's certainly not the end of the debate.

SEBASTIEN LE TOUX

1 Despite being the most decorated player in the brief history of the Philadelphia Union, Sebastien Le Toux has only played four seasons in Philadelphia. He is by far the youngest and has thus far garnered the fewest accolades of all the athletes in this book.

In spite of that, Le Toux is the Union's all-time leader in goals and assists, he scored the franchise's first goal, became its first All-Star, and recorded its only hat trick and only playoff goal. Along the way, he has become one of the most popular athletes in a city that is famously, gleefully hard on its superstars. In a city that booed Mike Schmidt and made Donovan McNabb a pariah, Le Toux enjoys near-universal popularity among fans. It's a little disconcerting, even for Le Toux himself.

"I don't know if everyone likes me," Le Toux said, "but I know I have a good popularity with the people. I've never had anybody being mean to me—I've always tried to be nice to them because they're always nice to me."

Being nice helps, but the source of Le Toux's popularity has as much to do with his accomplishments as with his attitude.

Sebastien Le Toux was born on January 10, 1984 in Mont-Saint-Aignan, France. He grew up in Rennes, a city of about 200,000 in Brittany, where he supported the local soccer club and tagged along with his older brother to play pickup games.

"It was a dream, I was just young," Le Toux said. "My first time was watching a game on TV; I wanted to be on the field one day. The first time I'd think about it, like, this was exactly what I want to do, was the first time my dad brought me to a live game in France. I was just sitting in the stands, I was too small I couldn't have a seat, so I was in the stairs, and I knew that I wanted one day to be on the field."

Le Toux came up as a right back in the youth academy at the local club, Stade Rennais FC, a middle-class club in the Ligue 1, the French first division. Le Toux wasn't offered a contract when he graduated from the Rennes academy, so at age 20, he signed a two-year deal with Lorient, a second-division club, where he played intermittently as the club won promotion in 2006.

As a free agent for the first time, Le Toux, then 22, took his career in a different direction entirely.

"I stayed eight months without contract, going here and there, with a few tryouts, but nothing really excited me," Le Toux said. "I didn't want to play third division."

In 2007, he picked up and moved to the Seattle Sounders, then playing in the USL, the second tier of American soccer, and moved to forward. For the first time, everything clicked.

"I got the opportunity to come to America for a tryout, and it was the first time I left France; I'd never gone outside France to play, and I just loved it," Le Toux said. "I love to speak English, I love the people here, the life, everything around . . . I don't know, it just made it so easy for me to decide that I wanted to stay here and play, even if the money was not the same as in Europe."

Le Toux was the USL's MVP his first season. He scored 24 goals in 54 games, and when the Sounders made the move up to MLS for the 2009 season, Le Toux was the first player they signed. Le Toux led the U.S. Open Cup in scoring in each of his three seasons with the Sounders, who reached the semifinals in 2007 and 2008 before winning it all in 2009.

His first season in MLS was a little less fortuitous. Seattle brought in Colombian phenom Freddy Montero and MLS veteran Nate Jaqua to play striker, forcing Le Toux into midfield, where he battled for playing time with former Sweden captain and Arsenal superstar Freddie Ljungberg. Suddenly on the periphery of the team, Le Toux scored only one goal in 28 games (15 starts) and found himself unprotected in the MLS Expansion Draft.

On the other side of the continent, the Union had taken notice.

Union manager Peter Nowak and top assistant John Hackworth, both former head coaches of US youth teams and assistants to Bob Bradley at the senior level, saw potential in Le Toux, even in spite of his uneven playing in 2009.

"We thought we were getting a player who had potential to score," said Hackworth, who succeeded Nowak as head coach and served in that capacity until June 2014. "Any time you can do it at a professional level, I think that's a really good sign. You always have to make a transition to the next higher level, but it's a difficult job to say, hey, this guy playing now is going to be this in the future."

While some MLS teams break the bank on high-profile international-level stars, the Union has always favored a more conservative approach. While Seattle, for instance, went after Ljungberg and former US international goalkeeper Kasey Keller for its first season, Philadelphia's biggest name was arguably the manager, Nowak, who'd won the MLS Cup as both a player and a manager. Nowak made notable moves for U.S. international defender Danny Califf, who became the club's first captain, as well as 2008 Olympians Chris Seitz and Michael Orozco. The big offensive names were first-round draft picks Jack McInerney and Danny Mwanga, both of whom were viewed as long-term prospects rather than immediate impact players.

"The first thing the coach, Peter Nowak, said when he picked me was 'We want to see you as a forward for our team.' It was a relief, that I could show again that I could play forward," Le Toux said.

Le Toux started at forward and played the full 90 minutes in the Union's first-ever game, a messy 2-0 loss away to Le Toux's old club, the Seattle Sounders. Two weeks later, he got the start for the Union's first-ever home game, which, because the team's purpose-built stadium in Chester hadn't been completed in time, was played in front of 34,870 fans at Lincoln Financial Field. Which brings us back to why Sebastien Le Toux is one of Philadelphia's most beloved athletes.

Sebastien Le Toux *(Vosie)*

"There was so much emotion in that day," Hackworth said. "I was living down at Dockside at the time and I went for a run through Old City, and nobody knew who I was, or I didn't think they knew. But every block, people were saying 'Good Luck!' or 'Go Union.' It was pretty cool, and it just kept building up toward the game."

The occasion wasn't lost on Le Toux either: "It was kind of amazing to walk around before the game, to see the stands empty. I remember coming onto the field and shaking the hand of Vice President Joe Biden, and you could see that the stands were kind of half full, half empty, and that was weird."

Once the game started, things only got crazier. Le Toux took a fifth-minute cross from Roger Torres and beat D.C. United goalkeeper Troy Perkins for the first goal in franchise history. He scored again in the 40th minute on a breakaway to double his league tally from the season before.

"When I scored the second goal," Le Toux said, "I didn't know why, but it would get louder. People told me after the game that lots of people got into the game after about 10 minutes, because they were late because of all the security and stuff."

United tied the game in the second half, but with 10 minutes to play, Le Toux completed his hat trick on a free kick. The Union held on for the first win in franchise history and the first chapter of a love affair between fans and player.

The home opener against United was also the coming-out party for the Union supporters' group, the Sons of Ben, who quickly came up with a tribute song for their new leading scorer.

"I know they have one," Le Toux said, "Because they sang it all the time in my first two years: Oh, Le Toux, Le Toux . . . something like You're Frencher than me or you . . . You'll score us a goal or two, or three—because of the hat trick. It's not very good lyrics, but it's the one I hear every time I see them."

To hear Le Toux tell it, he became the most popular player on the team more or less by default.

"I think that because this team was new," Le Toux said, "you need a player or two to be good for the team, so people can recognize the team because of those players. Like if I [say]: 'Galaxy,' you would say 'David Beckham' or '[Landon] Donovan.'"

Maybe. But Philadelphia sports fans love their own particular sports culture almost as much as they love the games themselves: they want an emotional investment. Their heroes aren't just great players; they also need to have Chase Utley's sneering self-confidence, Brian Dawkins' soul-baring emotion or Bobby Clarke's all-consuming desire to win, within or without the rules. Philadelphia fans are obsessed not only with winning and community, but also with making sure the athletes they cheer for understand the culture that supports them.

And while some Eagles fans might sneer at soccer, Union fans, as a group, are the same, only younger and dressed in scarves instead of shoulder pads.

Le Toux is a skilled player with keen vision, a good first touch, and a penchant for well-placed curling free kicks. He's tall and undeniably athletic, but like many soccer players, he's too skinny to be particularly imposing. Far from playing with the smoldering anger of Allen Iverson, for instance, Le Toux is relentlessly upbeat—Hackworth mentioned Le Toux's energy and optimism as one of his best qualities as a teammate. In person, he's extremely self-assured, but also polite, humble, and patient. Scoring goals will make you a fan favorite, but Le Toux also has a knack for dealing with passionate and demanding fans.

"Seba's a great ambassador for the club, in the way that he signs autographs and goes out of his way to be in the community," Hackworth said. "If anyone requested something of him, he really took it to heart. It says a lot about Seba, the way [he] interacts with fans."

But Le Toux is relentless on the field, and that, Hackworth says, is what sets him apart.

"Soccer is a game where sometimes it takes a long time to break down another team," Hackworth said. "And as the game gets later into the first half or second half, it seems like that's where Seba, he's just getting going, and that's where he really gets recognized.

"We have all these cool analysis tools now that we look at speed of a player, sprints, distance covered. What Seba does is he doesn't get slower as the game goes on. He can maintain his level throughout, and that's a fantastic thing for a player to do. It takes a lot of heart and determination, but it also takes a very fit athlete."

Le Toux finished 2010 as the Union's leading scorer, with 14 goals and 11 assists. Freddy Montero, his former Seattle teammate, was the only other player in MLS to reach double figures in both categories. Le Toux started the All-Star game that year and, along with the Union, built on that success in 2011. Veteran goalie Faryd Mondragon joined the team along with defender Carlos Valdez. Those two, along with Sheanon Williams, in his first full year as a starter, transformed what had been at times a calamitous backline into one of the league's best. The Union went 11-8-15, good for third in the Eastern Conference and the team's first-ever playoff berth. They lost to Houston Dynamo 3-1 on aggregate (the one goal was Le Toux's, of course), but the signs were good going into 2012.

That's when everything went wrong.

In January 2012, the Union brought Le Toux back from his offseason vacation to go on trial with the Bolton Wanderers of the English Premier League. Bolton, locked in a relegation battle, was looking for reinforcements in the winter transfer window and hoped Le Toux and New York Red Bulls defender Tim Ream could strengthen the team.

Le Toux, who had one year left on his contract and was more interested in an extension than a move back to Europe, was less than enthusiastic.

"I said, 'no, I don't want to,'" Le Toux said. "I talked a couple months [before] with [Union CEO] Nick Sakiewicz and he said he wanted to offer me a new contract. It's not about the money I could get over there—I want to stay in Philadelphia, I'm happy here, and I want to keep building this franchise."

Le Toux arrived in England jet-lagged and far from his midseason form. Almost immediately he picked up a foot injury and failed to impress. Nevertheless, Bolton's coaching staff wanted him to extend his tryout another week, but the day they were supposed to meet to discuss the extension, they were in London nailing down the terms of Ream's permanent transfer. Le Toux flew home the next day.

He returned to find Nowak furious that he'd cut short his trial. The disagreement led to the end of Le Toux's relationship with Nowak, who traded the franchise's first star to the Vancouver Whitecaps shortly after.

"[Nowak] really lied to my face, and I hate that," Le Toux said. "I'm very easy to forgive for whatever happened, if it's an honest mistake, but the fact that he really played with my career and my life, and the fact that I knew he wanted to sell me for money and never told me about it . . . If he'd come to me and said, 'Seba, it'd be great if we could sell you for this amount because the team needs money,' I'd say, 'Okay, but I want to stay here.'"

The fans, already confused and appalled by Le Toux's abrupt departure, weren't soothed by an incendiary interview Le Toux gave with Chris Vito of the *Delaware County Times* shortly after the trade, in which Le Toux said he'd retire rather than play for Nowak again.

"I left for a year and I know it was heartbreaking for me, and for [the fans] too," Le Toux said. "Like I tried to tell them, I didn't choose to leave like that—they sent me away. It was not my choice."

Le Toux's year away from Philadelphia wasn't without its positives, however. He scored only five regular-season goals between his stints in Vancouver and New York, but his time with the Red Bulls brought him together with a player he'd looked up to as a teenager: Thierry Henry.

Henry was a key member of the French national team when Les Bleus won the World Cup in 1998 and the European championship in 2000. Henry went on to become one of the world's greatest players in stints for Arsenal and Barcelona before joining the Red Bulls in 2010.

"It was very nice," Le Toux said. "I watched him on TV in my youth when he won the World Cup for France. I didn't know him personally, so it was a great occasion for me to see how he is as a man compared to as a soccer player. I knew he was a fantastic soccer player . . . and he is a great human being too."

Meanwhile, in Philadelphia, the progress that had been made in 2011 was reversed in 2012. Mondragon left before the season to finish his career in his home nation of Colombia, and during the season, Califf and Mwanga were traded away as well as the Union slid back toward the bottom of the table. By mid-June, Union ownership had fired Nowak and replaced him with Hackworth, who looked for a familiar face with whom to start rebuilding.

"One of the first things I thought about when I had the opportunity as the interim head coach was 'Can we get Seba back here?'" Hackworth said. "Sometimes these things are much clearer after the fact, but that was a move that I think if we, as an organization, had to do over again, we probably wouldn't do it."

Le Toux returned to Philadelphia about 10 months after he left, in exchange for allocation money and midfielder Josué Martínez. He found many things that were different. For one, his relationship with Hackworth was changed. Additionally, the team to which he returned was somewhat different.

For instance, McInerney had not only replaced Le Toux in the No. 9 jersey, but also he had cemented his place as the team's starting center forward.

"John likes to play a 4-3-3, which is a little bit different than what I like," Le Toux said. "I like to play in a 4-4-2 as a forward, but the way we play right now with all the good players we have in the midfield, we have more possession, so it's nice to receive more balls so I can finish in front of the goal."

Le Toux scored only three goals for the Union in 2013, but made up for it with a career-high 12 assists in his new supporting role. Even though he's not playing his preferred position, Le Toux isn't particularly bothered.

"My goal is not to score the most goals or to be the star of this team, but that every year we do well—at minimum, we make the playoffs."

Just past his thirtieth birthday, the age where outfield players tend to start slowing down, Le Toux embraces his role as a veteran leader and mentor for players like forward Andrew Wenger without considering the end of his own career ("Just because I'm thirty, maybe people say you're old, but I don't think you're old when you're thirty—I think you're old when you're sixty," he said), and intends to play at least five more years, more if possible, and preferably all in Philadelphia, the city he's adopted as his own.

"I can feel how much joy it brings to a sports town like Philadelphia when they can see their team makes the playoffs at minimum and comes back the next year," he said. "I hope to bring a title this year or in the next few years."

And maybe that's the key to Le Toux's popularity—not only does he play hard and play well, but also he wants to play in Philadelphia. Because if a city's going to love an athlete, it's always nice when the athlete loves the city back.

TOM GOLA

2 A common shorthand for calling a player popular is to say that he could run for mayor. Tom Gola came closer than anyone else on this list to bringing that aphorism to life.

Gola was born on January 13, 1933 in Philadelphia, the oldest of seven children of a Philadelphia policeman. His backstory is fairly unremarkable—Gola grew up playing pickup games and for La Salle College High in the Catholic League, but what is remarkable is the wide range of skills he developed as an amateur. Philadelphia basketball legend Sonny Hill called Gola one of the best high school players in city history, and his record backs up that claim, because as a boy, Gola won constantly.

Gola won a national schoolboy title with Incarnation of Our Lord and a city high school title with La Salle High, where he still holds the school scoring record. When the time came to choose a college, Gola stayed close to home, opting to play for the La Salle Explorers.

Gola was a four-year starter, thanks to a Korean War exemption that allowed La Salle to play freshmen on the varsity, and he took full advantage of the opportunity. The six-foot-six-inch

Gola started at center and led the Explorers in scoring (17.2 ppg) and rebounding (16.5 rpg), and led them to the NIT title as well, a somewhat more impressive feat when the NCAA Tournament only included 16 teams. After La Salle's 75-64 title game win over Dayton, Gola was named the tournament's co-MVP.

The next year, Gola's Explorers went 25-3 and returned to the NIT. The Explorers, as one of the top four seeds in the NIT that year, received a bye to the quarterfinals, but they suffered a one-point loss to St. John's in that round. Despite the disappointing postseason, Gola was named to his first All-America team.

In 1953–54, Gola took his next step forward: 23 points and 21.7 rebounds per game, a school-record 41 points in a single game, another first-team All-America selection, and his first NCAA Tournament appearance. Gola made it count, delivering the game-tying assist in their opening round overtime win over Fordham, then leading La Salle to its only national championship with more comfortable wins over N.C. State, Navy, Penn State, and Bradley. Gola was named the tournament's Most Outstanding Player, making him the only player in history, to this day, to be named MVP of the NIT and MOP of the NCAA Tournament.

La Salle went back to the national championship game in 1955, losing by 14 points to San Francisco, which had a center of their own—Bill Russell—who would go on to make something of himself in the future.

Gola still had a pretty good season regardless: 24.4 ppg, 19.9 rpg, and a third straight year as a consensus first-team

All-America player. La Salle coach Ken Loeffler described Gola and his more pedestrian teammates as "four students and one ballplayer," and stuck Gola with the nickname "Mr. All-Around."

Gola's collegiate career is fairly staggering to behold, even 60 years later. Gola led La Salle in scoring, rebounding, field goal percentage, and free throw percentage in each of his four seasons, finishing with a career line of 20.9 ppg and 18.7 rpg, and over four years, his Explorers teams went 102-19. Gola is still the NCAA's all-time leading rebounder, with 2,201 over his four years at La Salle.

Tom Gola was a territorial selection of the Philadelphia Warriors in 1955, which meant the local boy would continue to make good with the local team. When he joined the NBA at age 22, Gola switched positions from center to shooting guard, and his versatility was one of the most compelling reasons in support of his greatness. Gola had a very nice 10-season NBA career, but his career line (11.3 ppg, 8.0 rpg, 4.2 apg) calls to mind Evan Turner over, say, Hal Greer or Billy Cunningham, two outstanding Sixers players who didn't make this list.

Gola's nickname, Mr. All-Around, is pretty unimaginative as Philadelphia basketball nicknames go, not as cheeky as Chocolate Thunder or as evocative as The Answer or as mellifluous as Dr. J. But it's descriptive.

The NBA in 1955 wasn't much more exciting than Gola's nickname: it bore only a passing resemblance to anything we'd recognize as basketball. The shot clock beat Gola to the league by only a year, and at that point, the game was played mostly below the rim. The most dominant player of that era, George Mikan, was . . . well, I don't want to go describe Mikan as a smaller Greg Ostertag all on my own, so I'll quote Bill Simmons on him:

> "Calling someone the greatest pre-shot-clock-force is like calling One on One: Dr. J vs. Larry Bird the greatest computer game of the early eighties. In other words, you're not saying much. The six-foot-ten Mikan peaked with a tiny three-second lane, no shot clock, no seven-footers, no goaltending rules, and barely any black players . . . and it's not like he was putting up Wilt-like numbers."

In other words, those old crotchety guys who might wax poetic about how great the game was in the 1950s—if you ever catch one of them snarking on the WNBA, you have my permission to knock his prune juice on the floor, because men's basketball in the 1950s makes the WNBA look like NBA Jam.

In Gola's rookie year, 1955–56, the league as a whole shot 38.7 percent from the field. People who like to talk about solid fundamental basketball often forget that scoring is a fundamental part of basketball, too, and everybody was terrible at it in the 1950s.

This might sound more like an indictment of Gola than anything else, but Gola was one of the first players who helped bring the game into the modern era. Nowadays, positions in the NBA mean almost nothing. LeBron James can play any of the five positions, because he's a freak of nature, but small ball lineups, point forwards, stretch fours, and centers with three-point range have blurred the distinction. Yet Gola was one of the first players who was capable of defending anyone, and as such is often cited as a predecessor of sorts to Magic Johnson, himself a predecessor of James.

On offense, Gola shot 40 percent or better from the field and 72 percent or better from the line every year, which was more impressive then than it is now, and he emerged as a ball-handler and playmaker for the Warriors from the wing right from the get-go. In fact, one of college basketball's most prolific scorers ever seemed to be unconcerned with scoring as a pro.

"We had [Paul] Arizin and [Neil] Johnston when I got there," Gola said. "They were like the top two scorers in the league. Then Wilt came along. My job was to guard the opponents' best guard—Jerry West, Oscar Robertson, Bill Sharman—and be a playmaker."

Gola still had a reliable shot and the array of post moves that made him a 20-point scorer in college—he wasn't Hakeem Olajuwon or Kevin McHale on the block, but he could score when he needed to score. In terms of being a distributor, re-bounder, defensive stopper, and second or third offensive option, Gola was a player in the mold of Scottie Pippen or a latter-day Grant Hill.

Relative to his competition, Gola is one of the greatest college basketball players ever, but as a professional, his contribution is less tangible than it is historical.

Anyway, the Warriors got Gola as a territorial selection in 1955, and since the NBA's regional player allocation system of the time netted the Warriors not only Gola, but Arizin and Wilt Chamberlain as well, Philadelphia's first NBA team ended up taking almost unfair advantage.

Tom Gola *(La Salle College)*

In 1955–56, Gola played 68 games as a rookie, finishing second on the team in assists and third in rebounds as the Warriors went 45-27 to win the Eastern Division and a first-round bye. The Warriors beat the Syracuse Nationals (who would later become the 76ers) in a five-game Eastern Division Finals, then beat the Fort Wayne Pistons 4-1 in the NBA Finals. Gola averaged a double-double in the Finals and finished second on the Warriors in points, rebounds, and assists.

At 23, Gola became the first, and so far, only player to win the NIT, NCAA Tournament, and NBA championship.

Gola went on to become the John Cazale of the NBA, turning into one of the league's best background actors and a five-time All-Star, but always in the shadow of Arizin or Chamberlain. The 1956 title would be Gola's last as a player, but in his six seasons in Philadelphia, Gola's Warriors made the playoffs five times. Gola averaged at least 10 points and 9 rebounds, again, as a wing player, every year, peaking in 1959–60 with 15 ppg, 10.4 rpg, and 5.5 apg.

In 1962, months after Wilt Chamberlian's legendary 100-point game (Gola, for what it's worth, didn't play), the Warriors packed up and moved to San Francisco. Gola went with them briefly, but asked to be traded back closer to home. So 21 games into the 1962–63 season, the Warriors sent Gola to the New York Knicks for Kenny Naulls and Willie Sears. Gola commuted from his home in Fox Chase to Manhattan while he played for the Knicks.

Gola, who was a month away from turning 30 when he was traded, declined pretty soon after he arrived in New York. He remained an efficient scorer, but after averaging 37 minutes a game with Philadelphia, Gola saw his playing time drop in New York to 35 minutes a game in 1962–63, then to 29 the next year, then 22, then 15 in 1965–66. He retired after the 1965–66 season at age 33. He was elected to the Hall of Fame in 1976.

To say that Gola remained active in the city after his retirement is something of an understatement. Mere months after retiring from the NBA, he went into politics at the urging of

William Meehan, a former youth coach of Gola's who happened to be the head of the local Republican Party. Gola won election to the Pennsylvania House of Representatives in 1968, becoming the first state representative for the 170th District, which includes Rockledge, as well as parts of Abington and Northeast Philadelphia.

While serving in the legislature, Gola took on an interesting day job: coach of the La Salle Explorers.

Left in disarray and under NCAA sanction after the departure of head coach Jim Harding, La Salle went 23-1 in Gola's first year as coach, finishing the season ranked No. 2 in the country by the Associated Press, but unable to challenge John Wooden's UCLA team for the national title because of a postseason ban earned under Harding. Gola coached one more year and went 14-12 before leaving not only that job, but also the legislature, for a new political challenge.

In 1969, Gola ran for city controller as a Republican and won with 56 percent of the vote. Left to work with a Democratic mayor, Gola and District Attorney Arlen Specter, the other star of the Republican ticket, spent one tumultuous term in office before being voted out in 1973. He went on to work on Ronald Reagan's 1980 presidential campaign and serve as the regional administrator of the Department of Housing and Urban Development.

A decade later, Gola took one last shot at public office, a run for the Republican nomination for mayor. Gola certainly had name recognition, but lacked the backing of the Republican party apparatus and finished third in a three-way contest behind U.S. Representative Charles Dougherty and the eventual winner, John Egan, who was, at the time, president of the Philadelphia stock exchange. (The 1983 Democratic primary, in which Wilson Goode beat former two-term mayor Frank Rizzo by a 53-46 margin, was far more interesting, considering Rizzo's political history, which could be described as either "colorful" or "scandal-ridden," depending on how charitable you wanted to be.) After his primary defeat in 1983, Gola left public life for good, tending to various business interests.

The season after Gola's Explorers won the 1954 national championship, La Salle's men's basketball team moved off campus, bouncing from venue to venue until 1998, when the university christened a new on-campus fieldhouse: Tom Gola Arena.

Gola died on January 26, 2014, at the age of 81.

RON HEXTALL

3 Ron Hextall was born on May 3, 1964, in Brandon, Manitoba, Canada. As a young man, he went into the family business and did pretty well, which would be less remarkable if the family business wasn't NHL hockey. Hextall's father, grandfather, and uncle had all played in the NHL as forwards—his grandfather, Bryan, won a Stanley Cup and a scoring title with the Rangers—so when young Ron Hextall was growing up, hockey seemed like a natural choice.

Unlike his relatives, Ron Hextall came up as a goalie, where he was somewhat unusual. Even as late as the 1980s, youth teams tended to stick the worst skaters and smallest players in goal, where their disadvantages would be kept to a minimum. Hextall was neither small nor unskilled. Hextall stood six-foot-three and weighed 192 pounds as a player, giving him a forward's size, and the simple explanation of what set him apart from his peers is that he skated like a forward as well.

Those attributes didn't exactly make him an instant star. Hextall stayed home for junior, playing three seasons for the Brandon Wheat Kings of the Western Hockey League, where he started consistently, but excelled less consistently.

He posted a 5.71 GAA in 30 games as a 17-year-old, and then, in Brandon's foray into the postseason, allowed 16 goals in 103 minutes for a 9.32 playoff GAA. At season's end, the Flyers took a shot at the beanpole goalie, spending their sixth-round pick (No. 119 overall) on Hextall. The 1982 draft class was a relatively weak one for goalies—18 were chosen, all in the third round or later, and only three played even a minute in the NHL—and Hextall was the sixth goalie off the board. No one predicted the incredible and immediate success he'd have in the NHL.

Those of us who lived through the Michael Leighton and Ilya Bryzgalov eras might have a hard time understanding this, but the Flyers in the 1980s often had more good goaltending than they could use. As a result, there was no reason to rush an 18-year-old Hextall, who had struggled in junior to the pros, regardless of his pedigree. In the mid-1980s, the Flyers relied on a reliable tandem of young goalies: Bob Froese and Pelle Lindbergh, a Swede who grew up idolizing Bernie Parent and under Parent's tutelage, became the Flyers' first real European star. So the Flyers sent Hextall back to Brandon.

In 1982–83, Hextall played 44 games and allowed a goal roughly every 10 minutes, while Lindbergh finished seventh in the Vezina Trophy voting. Hextall improved somewhat in his final season of junior hockey, posting a 4.27 GAA in 46 games and leading the Wheat Kings to the division semifinals. For comparison, the WHL's top goaltender that year was Hextall's future Flyers teammate Ken Wregget, another

Brandon native who was the first goalie taken in Hextall's class. Wregget posted a 3.16 GAA in 1983–84.

By that point, Hextall had aged out of major junior, and the Flyers sent him to the minor leagues. He split 1984–85 between Kalamazoo of the IHL (where he went 6-11-1 with a 4.35 GAA) and the AHL's Hershey Bears, where he improved markedly: 4-6-0, 3.68 GAA. Lindbergh won the Vezina Trophy and backstopped the Flyers to the Stanley Cup Final, where they got beaten up badly by Wayne Gretzky and the Edmonton Oilers.

Hextall's only full year in Hershey was much better: a 3.41 GAA and five shutouts, but the Flyers suddenly suffered a shortage of goaltenders. On November 10, 1985, Lindbergh, leaving the Flyers' practice facility in Voorhees, New Jersey, was killed in a car accident, and the loss of the 26-year-old reigning Vezina winner resonates in the Flyers' community to this day. After winning the division again behind Froese, Darren Jensen, and veteran Chico Resch, the Flyers lost a close first-round series to the Rangers.

Hextall impressed head coach Mike Keenan in training camp and started and won the Flyers' regular-season opener, becoming the first third-generation NHL player. He never looked back from there, and quickly it became clear that the Flyers hadn't found just another goalie.

"Ron Hextall's skill set was something that we hadn't seen before in the NHL," said Jeff Marek of Rogers Sports Net. "He was entertaining, he was erratic, and in 1987 . . . he turned in one of the best goaltending performances we have ever seen."

In addition to being bigger than most goalies—Hextall stood eight inches taller than Lindbergh—he skated better and displayed comfort as a stickhandler that hadn't been seen before. Even then, most goalies were content to fish pucks out of the corners and generally stay home, but Hextall insisted on playing the entire defensive zone—he went into the corners to retrieve dump-and-chase passes so his defensemen wouldn't have to risk being hit, then unleashed rink-long outlet passes like Wes Unseld or Bill Russell would do on the basketball court. Hextall also skated out between the faceoff dots to retrieve backpasses from his defensemen, the way soccer goalies do. Hextall's 31 career assists rank eighth all-time among NHL goalies.

"If it was allowed, Ron Hextall should've joined the rush," Marek said. "He was such a great skater, such a great stickhandler, and he played in a lot of ways with a power forward's mentality."

That mentality manifested itself in two ways: first, his skill. Contrary to standard goaltender practice, Hextall used a curved stick, and on December 8, 1987, Hextall, with a two-goal lead over Boston and the Bruins' net empty, shot the puck the length of the ice and became the first NHL goalie to score from a direct shot.

The second way Hextall's power forward mentality shone through was his propensity for violence, a quality that obviously endeared him to the fans who had embraced the Broad Street Bullies a decade before. Before Hextall, goalies had fought, but Hextall turned his crease into a scene out of *A Clockwork Orange*. He was unafraid of facing down opposing forwards who lingered too long after he'd frozen the puck, or who buzzed the net or tapped him after the play. Hextall used his stick like a scimitar of justice, and he meted out retribution liberally on those who transgressed against him.

Hextall was involved in several violent incidents in the early years of his career. For starters, he poleaxed Edmonton tough guy Marty McSorley after a shove beside the net, and on another occasion jabbed Greg Adams in the face with the blade of his goalie stick. In practice for the 1987 Canada Cup, Hextall broke Sylvain Turgeon's arm with a slash, a remarkable event considering that Turgeon was one of Hextall's own defensemen. In the 1989 playoffs, Montreal defenseman Chris Chelios took a high, dirty hit on Brian Propp. Later in the series, Hextall chased Chelios into the corner and pounded him senseless like Scut Farkus in *A Christmas Story*. He was like Bobby Clarke in goalie gear.

In NHL history, a goalie has registered 50 PIMs or more 15 times. Five of those seasons are Hextall's, including the only three seasons of more than 70 PIMs by any NHL goalie: Hextall's first three seasons in the league, in which he recorded 104, 104, and 113 PIMs.

Which is not to say that Hextall wasn't a great NHL goaltender, immediately. Hextall arrived as a 22-year-old rookie on a Flyers team that had won two straight division titles and boasted perhaps the best defensive corps in franchise history: Hall of Famer Mark Howe, Brad McCrimmon, Brad Marsh,

Doug Crossman, and J.J. Daigneault. Up front, the Flyers had 58-goal scorer Tim Kerr to go with Propp, a 21-year-old Peter Zezel, and a 22-year-old Rick Tocchet, who not only registered 49 points, but also spent 288 minutes in the box.

Hextall claimed the starting job quickly, and by December 18, the Flyers had traded Froese for Kjell Samuelsson and a second-round pick. Hextall went on to lead the NHL in games, minutes, wins, shots faced, saves, and save percentage to take home the Vezina Trophy. Hextall's rate stats (.902 save percentage, 3.00 GAA) might not look impressive by today's standards, but the 1980s were the NHL's highest-scoring era—in Hextall's rookie year, 1986–87, the average NHL team scored 3.67 goals per game, compared to 2.57 in 2003–04 (the year before the lockout) and 2.74 in 2013–14. Save percentages are higher now too: a league average of .880 in 1986–87 compared to an all-time high of .914 in 2013–14. While Hextall's 1986–87 numbers would get him laughed out of the league today, they were immensely impressive back then.

The Flyers finished fourth in the NHL in goals scored and, behind their slash-happy rookie goalie, allowed the second-fewest goals in the NHL.

Hextall was spectacular through a difficult playoff run: each of the first three rounds went at least six games, and Hextall was the goalie of record every time. The Flyers eventually beat the Canadiens in six games to set up a rematch against the Oilers for the Stanley Cup.

Ron Hextall *(Jim Tyron)*

"The Oilers knew exactly what they were getting into," Marek said. "This was a great series because there wasn't much of a feeling out process—each team knew what the other team was all about."

Edmonton won the first two games at home, then the Flyers engineered the first comeback from 3-0 down in a Stanley Cup Final game, scoring five unanswered goals. In Game 4, Hextall had what would become his signature playoff moment.

"The Oilers, specifically, tried to get to Hextall: keep buzzing him, give him a little tap, give him a little bump, try to get Hextall off his game," Marek said. "And it finally reached a crescendo when Glenn Anderson skated by and gave him a little tap, and Hextall looked around, found the closest Oiler, and chopped down Kent Nilsson in front of his net in the slash heard 'round the world."

Hextall's slash on Nilsson was particularly vicious—he shifted both of his hands down to the knob and chopped down from his shoulder like a lumberjack swinging a baseball bat and caught Nilsson, who was miraculously uninjured, on the back of the legs with the edge of his blade. The Flyers lost 4-1, and while they came back to win the next two games and stave off elimination, Edmonton wrapped up the title at home in Game 7 with a 3-1 victory.

Hextall became the second Flyer to win the Conn Smythe Trophy for playoff MVP in a losing effort. Hextall became the first goalie to make more than 600 saves in a single playoff year (he made 698, a record that would stand for seven years), and the 769 shots he faced are the third-most in NHL history.

Hextall came back the next year eight games late, thanks to a suspension he incurred for his slash on Nilsson, and experienced a minor sophomore slump: 3.50 GAA, .886 save percentage, as the Flyers finished the season 15 points worse without McCrimmon, who'd been traded to Calgary. Additionally, Kerr was limited to eight games thanks to a shoulder injury that also cost him the 1987 Stanley Cup Final.

The 1988–89 season was more of the same, though despite finishing in the last Patrick Division playoff spot with only 80 points, the Flyers went all the way to the conference finals, where they jumped out to a 1-0 lead over the 115-point Montreal Canadiens before losing the series 4-2. On the way,

Hextall scored his second career goal—a shorthanded goal against the Capitals—the first playoff goal by an NHL goalie.

That was the last happy season in Hextall's first Philadelphia go-around. He missed almost all of the 1989–90 season because of injuries and a contract dispute, and when he came back in 1990–91, he spent the next two years in a platoon with Wregget and outside the playoffs.

After the 1992 season, Hextall found himself on his way out of Philadelphia as part of the monster package sent to the Quebec Nordiques in exchange for Eric Lindros. Hextall quickly established himself as the starter in Quebec City, appearing in 54 games and playing well in Quebec's first-round loss to Patrick Roy and the eventual champion Canadiens, the same team and goalie who had beaten Hextall in his previous playoff action, the 1989 Eastern Conference Finals.

In 1993, the NHL expanded again to include the Mighty Ducks of Anaheim and the Florida Panthers. Quebec, able to protect only one goalie in that year's expansion draft, chose 22-year-old Stephane Fiset over Hextall, and rather than lose him for nothing, traded Hextall to the New York Islanders, where he enjoyed his greatest success since his rookie year. Hextall started 65 games and posted an .898 save percentage and a 3.08 GAA, but on the eve of the 1994–95 season, Hextall was traded a third time.

Bobby Clarke had feuded with Hextall over contract issues in 1989, but after his firing in 1990 and rehiring in 1994, Clarke brought Hextall back, along with a sixth-round pick, for goalie Tommy Soderstrom. The start of that season was delayed by a three-month lockout, but Hextall returned to a starter's role, if not the workhorse role he'd enjoyed in his early 20s. Hextall backstopped the 1995 Flyers' run to the Eastern Conference Finals, then posted career bests in save percentage (.913) and GAA (2.17) in 1995–96. In 1996–97, the Flyers, who were by this point leaning more heavily on backup Garth Snow, finished second in the Atlantic Division, then reached the Stanley Cup Final easily, marking Hextall's second trip there in a decade.

During the 1997 playoffs, the Flyers switched off between Hextall and Snow, though neither was of much help in the Stanley Cup Final: an embarrassing sweep at the hands of the Detroit Red Wings.

"I think the final nail in the coffin for a lot of people was that 1997 Stanley Cup Final and the Garth Snow–Ron Hextall swap," Marek said. "No one could figure out what Terry Murray was doing with his netminders. And it seemed like Terry Murray would hear a whisper from Ed Snider and immediately change his mind about his goaltending."

Hextall played 46 games the next year, but managed only one playoff appearance in relief of Sean Burke. The next summer, Clarke signed John Vanbiesbrouck, who relegated Hextall to 23 appearances, though the 34-year-old registered the last two assists of his career, his first in three years. The Flyers waived him at season's end, and when nobody claimed him, Hextall retired that September at the age of 35.

Hextall's prime and career overall were relatively short, in large part because of Patrick Roy and Roy's goaltending coach, François Allaire. In 1986, Roy, a 20-year-old rookie, arrived in Montreal and lived out a similar story to the one Hextall produced the next year, the unorthodox rookie goalie carrying his team through to the Stanley Cup Final.

Roy's innovation, however, was the butterfly style. Up until his arrival, NHL goalies, including Hextall, played a stand-up style, remaining on their skates in most cases and kicking out or using their stick to block shots. Roy and those who followed would position themselves on their shins, splaying their leg pads out and using that bulk, as well as their chest, blocker, and trapper to cover as much of the net as possible before the shot, therefore reducing the shooter's target space. It revolutionized the game, and almost every goalie in the league today plays a variation on the butterfly.

"It was the François Allaire-ing of the NHL," Marek said, "when everybody decided that they had to change from being a traditional stand-up goaltender to covering everything down low and having a tight core and keeping your shoulders back and making your shoulders big and blocking shots instead of making saves. It almost felt as if Hextall became one of the last of a dying breed."

Stand-up goalies like Hextall either evolved to fit the new system or died out. When Hextall entered the league in 1986, he acted like a sixth skater, taking advantage of his skill and upright positioning to influence the game even when he wasn't stopping pucks. Unfortunately, he almost immediately found himself on the wrong end of a revolution in the other direction, one in which goalies stay close to home and never go into the corner for pucks—in fact, Hextall's roving style would now be illegal, thanks to the trapezoid rule.

After his career was over, Hextall followed the path of several Flyers players who came before him, such as Clarke, Bill Barber, and Paul Holmgren, and joined the Flyers' front office as a scout. After seven years, Hextall followed another Flyers scout, Dean Lombardi, across the country to Los Angeles, where the Kings had hired Lombardi to be their GM, and Lombardi, in turn, hired Hextall to be his assistant. By the start of the 2011–12 season, the Kings had developed a distinctly Philadelphian flavor, with Lombardi and Hextall in the front office, former Flyers head coaches Terry Murray and John Stevens on the coaching staff, and Mike Richards, Justin Williams, and Simon Gagne on the active roster. In midseason, Lombardi fired Murray and replaced him with Darryl Sutter (Stevens stayed on as an assistant) and traded for another former Flyer, Jeff Carter, to bolster the team's offense. The Kings won their first Stanley Cup with relative ease, and Hextall, in his sixth season as assistant GM, won his first ring.

A year later, Hextall returned to Philadelphia to serve as Holmgren's assistant, and on May 7, 2014, Hextall was named general manager of the Flyers.

CHUCK BEDNARIK

4 When you become accustomed to the high-speed, up-tempo spread offense version of football, you get sore imagining someone playing all 60 minutes of an NFL game. Sure, we still have two-way players today—you'll see Julian Edelman take the odd snap at nickel corner, and at the college level it's not unusual for a particularly talented defensive back to return kicks, line up at receiver, and quarterback the team's Wildcat package.

But what Chuck Bednarik did was different. First, no modern two-way players are playing every snap on both sides of the ball. Second, playing cornerback and receiver means a lot of running, but playing center and middle linebacker all at once means more contact and therefore more wear-and-tear. Third, today's NFL is more violent than Bednarik's (save your "back when men were real men" get-off-my-lawn-ism . . . players are bigger and faster now than they were in the 1950s, which means they hit harder just based on simple physics, and higher standards of organization and professionalism mean they're coached better as well). Bednarik was listed at six feet three inches, 234 pounds, almost exactly the same size as an offensive lineman that Seattle Seahawks safety Kam Chancellor is listed at today. However, modern NFL players have access to some of the best medical care in the world. Bednarik and his contemporaries had painkillers and flimsy helmets that you wouldn't trust to protect a child from a bicycle accident.

Some people find heroism in the utter disregard for safety and misunderstanding of injuries that was endemic to the pre-merger NFL, that it harkens back to an era where men were men and whoever wasn't stricken with polio was stronger, mentally and physically, than today's pro football players, much less ordinary people.

I don't know if it's heroic—"crazy" is the word I'd choose—but it's absolutely impressive.

Bednarik was the last of the full-time two-way players, which meant he was in the trenches to the end of his career, against younger athletes who took half the game off. That distinction is the foundation for a legend so astounding that there's a small part of me that wonders if Bednarik was even real, or if he was constructed as a mythical hero, either to exemplify a certain ethic, like Achilles or Beowulf, or as an elaborate prank on everyone who is too young to remember the NFL before the Super Bowl.

The more you dive into the legend of Chuck Bednarik, the more you realize he embodied the pre-merger NFL, the tough guy football player and the hard-nosed blue-collar Philadelphian. So much so that as you learn about Bednarik, you expect to hear that he carried a sword that was given to him by the Lady of the Lake, and that he parked his blue ox outside Franklin Field on game days.

The legend starts, as do most legends, with an unassuming, working-class local kid. Bednarik was born to Slovak immigrants on May 1, 1925. Bednarik, who learned to speak English at the local parochial school, quickly became a standout three-sport athlete and could as easily have been a pro baseball player as a football player.

But like most young men his age, he was called off to war after turning 18. Bednarik was a waist gunner on a B-24 bomber, one of the most dangerous assignments in the American military, as the daylight raids over Germany subjected bomber crews not only to attacks from fighter aircraft but to ground-based anti-aircraft fire as well—casualty rates for bomber crews were the highest of any branch of the American military during World War II. In an interview for the National World War II Museum, Bednarik said he never shot down an enemy plane, but he came back from Europe after 30 missions as a highly-decorated 20-year-old, with the Air Medal (with four oak leaf clusters) and four Battle Stars to his credit.

While Bednarik remained proud of his Slovak heritage, the war hero became and remained intensely patriotic throughout his life.

"I want to thank the Almighty God for having my parents migrate to this country from Czechoslovakia," Bednarik said in his Hall of Fame induction speech, "and having me raised up as a good American boy and I'm just happy that I'm an American."

Bednarik returned home in 1945 and, after growing up assuming he'd work in the mines for U.S. Steel, like his father and most of his hometown, found himself at the University of Pennsylvania, thanks to the G.I. Bill.

It was at Penn where Bednarik took his first steps toward Philadelphia sports immortality. When constructing this list, I focused almost entirely on the professional careers of these 20 athletes, and didn't go out of my way to look for players who grew up in the Delaware Valley or attended local universities before turning pro—in fact, Bednarik is one of only three athletes listed here who made any mark on Philadelphia-area sports as an amateur. By comparison, six of these 20 were raised outside the United States. But as Bednarik was fond of making an impact on things—the Wehrmacht, Frank Gifford, and so on—he made his presence felt as a Quaker. After sitting out 1945 (freshmen weren't allowed to play varsity sports at that point), Bednarik was named Penn's starting center early in the 1946 season, and went on to be named All-America as Penn went 6-2 and finished the season ranked 13th in the nation. Bednarik was once again named to the All-America team as a junior, and played linebacker on a defense that allowed only 35 points all year (Penn dropped 59 on Lafayette on Opening Day). The Quakers finished the season 7-0-1, the lone blemish on their record a 7-7 tie against Army, and were ranked No. 7 in the country at year's end.

Bednarik's best season was his senior year. While Penn regressed to 5-3 (losing to Penn State, Army, and Cornell after starting the season 5-0), the Quakers' star two-way player not only brought home All-America honors for the third time in three seasons, but also he won the Maxwell Award as the top college football player in the country and finished third in Heisman Trophy voting, which was as impressive an achievement for a linebacker/center then as it would be now: the other seven vote-getters that year were all quarterbacks and running backs, and the award has been as slanted in favor of those positions more or less since its inception. Bednarik was elected to the college football Hall of Fame in 1969, and in 1995, the Maxwell Football Club began handing out the Chuck Bednarik Award to the nation's best defensive player.

Bednarik, already a war hero/local boy-made-good/Ivy Leaguer/Gary Cooper figure, went first overall to the Eagles in the 1949 draft. He was only the second offensive lineman ever taken with the first pick. Bednarik played 10 games, starting seven, as the Eagles went 11-1 and won their second straight NFL championship, a phrase that sounds very strange to modern fans; but if Bednarik was real, then so was that title.

In 1950, Bednarik moved into the starting lineup at both center and linebacker, and from there his career really took off: Bednarik was named to the first of five consecutive Pro Bowls and five consecutive first-team All-NFL teams.

Part of the legend of Bednarik is that his record survives almost entirely on reputation. This isn't because, like some players, he's been imbued after the fact with metaphysical powers of will or motivation or clutchness—it's because NFL statistics as we know them now didn't exist in the 1950s. Forget about modern stats; the NFL didn't even record tackles and sacks in Bednarik's day—judging Bednarik, a linebacker and center, on solely on his statistical record would be like judging Bill Russell's career if the NBA didn't track rebounds. That said, Bednarik's statistical record, such as it is, is impressive.

Chuck Bednarik *(AP Photo)*

As is common in the biographies of legendary Philadelphia athletes, Bednarik's résumé contains a lengthy playoff drought. However, in addition to NFL titles in 1949 and 1960, the Eagles also led the NFL in scoring defense in 1950.

Bednarik's best season was 1953, when he intercepted a career-high six passes and ran one back for the only touchdown of his career. He also finished third in the NFL with four fumble recoveries, all the while playing center in addition to linebacker, and 10th in the NFL in average punt yardage.

In 1957, Bednarik made his seventh Pro Bowl in nine NFL seasons, and was named first-team All-NFL by the *Sporting News* and the *New York Daily News*, and second-team All-NFL by the AP, UPI, and the Newspaper Enterprise Association. He also missed his first game since his rookie season, and for the 1958 season, new Eagles coach Buck Shaw made his 33-year-old two-way star an offensive player only.

The Eagles dropped to 2-9-1, then rebounded to win seven games the next year. Finally, in 1960, Shaw called on the 35-year-old Bednarik to play both ways once more.

Up to that point, Bednarik was a mere mortal. By all accounts, an outstanding two-way player and a deserving Hall of Famer, but not a legend. Because no satisfactory data exist to tell Bednarik's story, we're forced to rely on anecdotes, and the three most important things to happen to Bednarik's reputation all took place in 1960.

First, Philadelphia *Bulletin* columnist Hugh Brown stuck a nickname on Bednarik. As you might have noticed—and as Bednarik, now in his 80s, will tell anyone who will listen nowadays—professional athletes didn't get paid a whole lot in the 1950s, certainly not as much as they do today, so many of them had offseason jobs to supplement their NFL salaries. So in the offseason, Bednarik worked for the Warner Company selling ready-mix concrete.

It's details like this that make me think Bednarik didn't actually exist, because any real football player renowned for his toughness and dour workmanlike nature wouldn't *literally* sell concrete in the offseason. He'd have worked construction or sold muscle cars or something adequately macho, but the Legend of Bednarik probably includes his offseason concrete sales job because saying he hunted wolves with his bare hands to make ends meet was just on the wrong side of ridiculous.

Nevertheless, Brown called Bednarik "as hard as the concrete he sells," and called the future Hall of Famer "Concrete Charlie."

That's a Hall of Fame nickname, perhaps the best sobriquet in Philadelphia sports folklore. In fact, in their 2006 book *The Great Book of Philadelphia Sports Lists*, WIP hosts Glen Macnow and Big Daddy Graham ranked "Concrete Charlie" the fourth-best nickname in Philadelphia sports history. And I think that's even too low. It's alliterative, affectionate, creative, and entirely relevant not only to Bednarik the player, but also Bednarik the man. "Concrete Charlie" even *sounds* tough.

The second legendary Bednarik moment came on November 20, 1960, when Bednarik delivered a devastating hit on Giants running back Frank Gifford. This hit was of the type that makes certain sportswriter types chitter gleefully at the days where NFL players invited serious real-life physical peril by running crossing routes. It's one of the most famous images of the pre-merger NFL, Gifford lying unconscious on his back on the Yankee Stadium turf, having suffered a concussion—and, Gifford would learn years later, a fractured vertebra—that would keep him in a hospital bed for several days and out of football for 18 months. Even at 35, seemingly playing out the string, Bednarik was capable of acts of startling force on the football field, the kind of hits that would later turn the likes of Jack Tatum and Bill Romanowski into pariahs and make James Harrison look like Asante Samuel.

The final signature Bednarik moment was the 1960 NFL Championship Game, which pitted the 10-2 Eagles against the 8-4 Green Bay Packers in a battle of future Hall of Fame quarterbacks (Bart Starr and Norm Van Brocklin).

Bednarik was the only player on the field to go the distance on both sides of the ball, playing just over 58 minutes and resting only on special teams. It wasn't a sterling performance by the Eagles—Green Bay jumped out to a 6-0 lead on two Paul Hornung field goals, then answered a field goal and a Tommy McDonald receiving touchdown with a 7-yard Max McGee score to lead 13-10 in the fourth quarter.

The Eagles defense gave up 401 yards—223 of them on the ground, largely to Hall of Famers Hornung and Jim Taylor—on a frozen, sloppy Franklin Field surface.

The Eagles, despite being outgained by more than 100 yards and suffering three turnovers to Green Bay's one, answered McGee's touchdown with a 58-yard return by rookie running back Ted Dean to get the ball into Packers territory, and Dean capped the ensuing drive with a five-yard score with 5:21 left.

Starr, down four points, started eating up yardage, culminating, with about 20 seconds left, in a short pass over the middle to Taylor. Taylor muscled through a tackle, but met Bednarik just inside the 10 yard line, and Concrete Charlie brought him down for good.

According to legend, Bednarik, after holding Taylor down as the final seconds ticked off the clock, had some final words for the Packers' running back. As time expired, he allegedly said, "You can get up now, Taylor, this fuckin' game's over."

It was the last game Eagles coach Buck Shaw would ever coach, the last championship the Eagles won to date, and the only playoff loss of Vince Lombardi.

Bednarik played two more seasons with the Eagles, missing out on a return trip to the NFL Championship Game by half a game in 1961, then going 3-10-1 in 1962. He retired at age 37 and was inducted to the Pro Football Hall of Fame in 1967. The Eagles have since retired his No. 60, and in 1987, Bednarik was inducted to the inaugural class of the Philadelphia Eagles Hall of Fame.

RICHIE ASHBURN

5 As far as we know, no major league team in any sport in the history of mankind has ever lost more games than the Phillies. Taken at face value, that's another piece of trivia that Philadelphia fans wear with a kind of ironic pride, along with the 25-year title drought, as an explanation for our comportment. Being a Philadelphia fan means being stroke-inducingly angry about four percent of the time, unabashedly exuberantly euphoric one percent of the time, and just kind of mildly peeved for the other 95 percent. Not heartbroken, but just kind of annoyed, as if you were looking forward to taking a date out for dinner at a nice restaurant, but he or she had to reschedule (not cancel altogether—tonight's just not a great night) and now instead of that juicy filet, you're eating peanut butter and jelly because that's the only food you have in your house. It should be noted, though, that no North American professional team has played for so long in one city under one name.

The good news is that if you're reading this, the Phillies' 10,000-plus losses probably didn't cause you that much pain: since 1976, the Phillies have been one of the more successful franchises in the game: in the past 38 years, the Phillies have won five pennants and two World Series and boasted multiple MVPs and Cy Young winners—hardly a total worthy of the Yankees or Cardinals, but not exactly the Milwaukee Brewers either.

Which makes that pre-1976 era all the more astounding: from the creation of the World Series in 1903 to the divisional era, starting in 1969, the Phillies took part in only two World Series, and that era wasn't exactly overflowing with near-misses: that era included only six seasons in which the Phillies finished within 10 games of the league leader. From the end of World War I to the end of World War II, the Phillies had one winning season, a 78-76 effort in 1932 in which they finished fourth, 12 games behind the Cubs.

Of course, in 1948, the Phillies brought up a twenty-one-year-old center fielder from Tilden, Nebraska, and he quickly became the best player on the best team in franchise history.

Richie Ashburn was a leadoff hitter out of central casting, the kind of player who would be at home at the top of a lineup at pretty much any point in history. The traditional leadoff hitter was a line-drive hitter with good speed and bat control, but not so much power that it would be a waste to put him at the top of a lineup rather than in the middle, where he could drive others in. Willie Mays, for instance, had all the skills of a leadoff hitter, but if you can hit 40 or 50 home runs, you're probably batting third or fourth.

The traditional leadoff hitter had to put the ball in play a lot, and once he was on base, had to be a threat to steal bases. Because a lot of smaller, faster players with little power tended to play second base, shortstop, or center field, some managers started (and sadly, continue) to use exclusively players from those positions at the top of the lineup, whether they could hit or not.

Ashburn could hit. And run. After signing with the Phillies out of high school in 1945, Ashburn spent two full seasons in the minors before coming to camp in 1948 as the team's third-string center fielder. The Phillies' starting center fielder, Harry Walker, the reigning batting champion, held out that spring, and when backup Charley Gilbert was hurt, Ashburn stepped into the Opening Day lineup and stayed there for twelve years.

Then just twenty-one years old, Ashburn hit a team-high .333 and stole a league-leading 32 bases. As a center fielder whose two home runs hardly made him middle-of-the-order material, Ashburn was set as the Phillies' leadoff hitter for the next decade, and along with pitcher Robin Roberts, became one of the franchise's first stars.

Over the past twenty years or so, the thinking has changed when it comes to who bats leadoff. No longer is it enough to be a fast guy with decent bat control who plays up the middle, because strategy has changed to treasure outs above all else. In Ashburn's day, the leadoff hitter would hit a single, then steal second base, at which point the No. 2 hitter would either bunt or hit a ground ball to the right side to move him to third, at which point the No. 3 hitter would hit a sacrifice fly to drive him in.

Nowadays, everyone has to hit, and the leadoff hitter doesn't just have to be able to run, but also he has to avoid making outs. As it turns out, Ashburn was not only one of the best baserunners in Phillies history, but one of the best at avoiding outs as well.

Ashburn led the National League in batting average twice, but he also led the league in on-base percentage four times, including a .441 OBP in 1954 and a .449 OBP in 1955. It's difficult to overstate the impact a player with Ashburn's speed has at the top of a lineup when he's on base that often, even in an era where the average OBP in the National League was in the mid-.330s, or about 20 points higher than it is today. In 1954, for instance, Ashburn hit second behind third baseman Willie "Puddin' Head" Jones for about half the season. Jones was a fine hitter, possessed of a superb nickname, but in the leadoff spot that year, Jones posted a .329 OBP. Ashburn's OBP as a leadoff hitter that year was .442, and when he was the first batter of the inning, he posted a .480 OBP. Over the course of a full season, let's say, 650 plate appearances for a leadoff hitter[2], Ashburn would reach base 74 times more often than Jones would. That's 74 more times where the heart of the order—it was usually Del Ennis driving Ashburn in, but it could be anyone—would come up with an extra man to drive in with a home run. Not only that, but that's 74 extra outs that players lower in the order could use up.

And for a player with Ashburn's speed and baserunning acumen, simply being on base was license to advance. Players with great speed and limited power are often said to have "invisible power," by virtue of being able to stretch singles into doubles and so on, or even to take liberties on the bases that allow them to get into scoring position without anyone behind them so much as making contact. Nowadays, you'll

---

2 Ashburn batted 703 times in 1954, Jones 610, so let's meet at a round number somewhere in the middle.

see that kind of thing said about players like Billy Hamilton and Ben Revere, neither of whom walk nearly as much as did Ashburn, but Ashburn was similar. A batter, particularly a leadoff batter, has no more important job to do than to get on base, and Ashburn was on base constantly.

The speed played up on both sides of the ball—Ashburn led all National League outfielders in range factor (putouts + assists/games played) in 10 of his first 11 seasons in the league, and he finished second the other year. To this day, Ashburn has the second-highest career mark in baseball history.

As a player alone, stripped of his historical significance, the best way to describe Ashburn is that he was the archetype of a great leadoff hitter by anyone's definition.

In 1949, the Phillies won 81 games, their highest total since 1917. That's worth thinking about for a moment, because while every team has rough stretches, it's hard to conceive of a major league ballclub being so consistently inept that they could go 32 years between 80-win seasons.

Nevertheless, the Phillies were clearly a team on the rise: Ashburn and another 21-year-old rookie, Robin Roberts, came up in 1948. Del Ennis, 24 on Opening Day 1950, had hit 55 home runs in 1948–49 and would add a career high 31 more in 1950. Andy Seminick and Stan Lopata would have been one of the best catchers in baseball if they were one person. Curt Simmons, a 21-year-old former bonus baby, was a reliable No. 2 starter behind Roberts until his National Guard unit was called up for active duty in Korea in September (consider for a moment how ridiculous it would seem today if a key pitcher in a pennant race got called off to go to war).

The final piece of the puzzle was Jim Konstanty, a slightly putsy, bespectacled 33-year-old journeyman reliever who put together a remarkable 1950, leading the league in appearances and saves and earning nearly 5 WAR and the MVP award for his effort.

The Phillies were still rank outsiders coming into 1950— they'd finished 16 games behind the Dodgers the year before, as was customary at the time—and they started slowly. A May 5 loss to St. Louis dropped them to 8-8, and from that point on, they turned it on. The Phillies won six straight and nine of 10, took over first place on May 11, and went absolutely gang-busters from that point until mid-September. From August 11 to September 15, Ashburn hit .364/.399/.443 with eight stolen bases and more extra-base hits (nine) than strikeouts (six). September 15 was a doubleheader. The Phillies won the first game 2-1 in one hour, 42 minutes. In the second game, the Phillies came from five runs down in the seventh inning to win 8-7 in a 19-inning marathon that lasted nearly three times that long. That doubleheader sweep put the Phillies 7 ½ games up on Brooklyn with two weeks to play. That win capped a 78-45 run and made the Phillies roughly 32-to-1 favorites to win their first pennant since 1915.

But whether due to Simmons' absence or having to play 28 innings in one day, they nearly gave it all up—the Phillies ended the season with a two-game series in Brooklyn, their once-secure lead now down to two games with two to play.

The Dodgers took the first game to set up a season finale between Roberts and Don Newcombe, perhaps the two best National League starting pitchers of that time.

With the score tied at one, Brooklyn's Cal Abrams started the bottom of the ninth with a walk, then moved to second on Pee Wee Reese's single to bring Duke Snider to the plate with the winning run 180 feet away.

Snider singled to center field, where Ashburn—who, while a very good defensive center fielder, was by no means possessed of Roberto Clemente's throwing arm—collected the ball and threw Abrams out at home by 10 feet. Roberts walked Jackie Robinson intentionally, then retired Carl Furillo and Gil Hodges to send the game to extra innings. That Roberts, who hadn't retired a batter in the inning, took care of Furillo and Hodges with the bases loaded and no room for error, might be more impressive, but Ashburn's season-saving throw is the legendary moment that sticks out in Phillies folklore as having won the pennant. Dick Sisler's home run in the top of the 10th inning got the Phillies across the finish line.

The World Series was a disaster—Ashburn went 3-for-17 in the only four playoff games he'd ever take part in, and the Phillies lost in four straight, though to be fair, the Yankees won the World Series pretty much every year at that point in history, and the Phillies as a team hit .203 in their only postseason appearance between 1915 and 1976. Getting there was a rare enough occurrence that it seems impolite to single out Ashburn for special blame.

While 1950 was Ashburn's most legendary season, it wasn't his best. In 1951 and 1958, Ashburn finished seventh in MVP voting, and in that span, he made the lion's share of his Hall of Fame case: three All-Star appearances, 1,545 hits, 686 walks, and 47.6 WAR in those eight seasons. Ashburn was not only great, but also he was consistent, playing 150 or more games in seven of those years and leading the league in plate appearances four times—an impressive mix of quality and quantity for a franchise that had seen embarrassingly little of both in the previous decades.

Richie Ashburn *(AP Photo)*

In 1959, at age 32, Ashburn finally slipped, suffering a drop of more than 200 points in his OPS and earning him a trade to the Cubs, where he rebounded for a year, once again leading the league in walks and OBP, before finishing his career with the Mets in 1962, where he became the only All-Star on the worst team in baseball history. Ashburn retired at age 35 with 2,574 career hits, 1,198 walks, 234 stolen bases, and 63.4 wins above replacement. Upon his retirement, Ashburn embarked on a second career as a broadcaster, where he spent the final 36 years of his life doing color commentary for Phillies games, the last 27 of them with Harry Kalas, with whom he formed one of the most beloved broadcasting partnerships in the country. In 1979, Ashburn's No. 1 became the second uniform number to be retired by the Phillies, and in 1995, he was elected to the Hall of Fame.

Ashburn, who was sometimes called "Whitey" as a player, because every blond-haired ballplayer in the 1950s was called "Whitey," was almost as popular for his folksiness and his on-air partnership with Kalas, who expanded Ashburn's moniker to "His Whiteness." Kalas and Ashburn became, collectively, a surrogate uncle to just about every Phillies fan born between 1965 and 1985 as the two called Phillies games (and famously ordered pizza to the booth while on the air) for 27 years.

Thanks in part to a broadcasting career that lasted more than twice as long as his playing career, Ashburn accumulated almost as many career anecdotes as stolen bases. Here are three of the best:

• During a game on August 17, 1957, Ashburn hit a woman named Alice Roth with a foul ball and broke her nose. In the same at-bat, Ashburn fouled off another pitch and hit Roth again while she was being carried out of the stands on a stretcher. Subsequently, Ashburn invited Roth and her sons to come visit the Phillies' clubhouse, and the two remained friends for years.

- While playing for the Mets in 1962, Ashburn found himself unable to call off shortstop Elio Chacon on fly balls to shallow center field. Chacon, a native of Venezuela, spoke no English and couldn't understand his teammates when they were calling for a ball. Once this became a recurring issue, Ashburn learned the Spanish phrase for "I've got it!" ("Yo la tengo!") and the next time a ball was hit behind second base, he successfully called off Chacon in the shortstop's native language. What Ashburn failed to account for was that his left fielder, Frank Thomas, didn't speak Spanish, at least until Thomas failed to respond to the call of "Yo la tengo" and ran Ashburn over.

- Ashburn was named MVP of the Mets that year, and as a token of gratitude, the organization gave the retiring Ashburn a 24-foot boat, which, sure enough, sank while docked in Ocean City, N.J.

All of these things—the fun stories, the broadcasting career, the historical context—have elevated Ashburn to legendary status among Phillies fans. When Citizens Bank Park opened in 2004, the main concourse was named Ashburn Alley in his honor. That reputation makes Ashburn extremely difficult to evaluate objectively as a player. As a player alone, is Ashburn really one of the top five Phillies players ever, or (to be more germane to this question), is he really one of the top 20 Philadelphia athletes of all time?

I'll answer this way. Nobody's a bigger Sliding Billy Hamilton fan than I am, but baseball before 1900 was barely baseball (in fact, I have a hard time comparing modern baseball to anything that happened before integration), so he's hard to evaluate, as are other Dead Ball Era players like Ed Delahanty and Sam Thompson.

Post-1920, Ashburn is third among Phillies players in career WAR, third in games played, third in runs scored, third in hits, sixth in stolen bases, 11th in batting average (minimum: 1,000 plate appearances) and fifth in OBP.

Where you place him among Phillies players depends on what you value and how you evaluate it. Does Ashburn's higher peak outweigh Jimmy Rollins' greater longevity against better competition? Does Ashburn's post-playing career service outweigh the fact that Bobby Abreu was probably a better player, even relative to his competition? One of the central problems I encountered, since this is a book meant to appeal to a city's fan base, and is therefore necessarily subjective, was whether to give out extra credit for things such as Ashburn's broadcasting career, and if so, how much. As a result, I'm not sure Ashburn had a better Phillies career, objectively, than Abreu or Rollins. Or even that, as a player alone, he's more deserving than Randall Cunningham or Hal Greer, and if you'd have one of those guys on this list, I wouldn't argue with you. But Ashburn's broadcasting career and the esteem he's held to this day breaks the tie.

ERIC LINDROS

6 I had been a hockey fan for more than a decade before it dawned on me how not normal Eric Lindros was.

At school and around the neighborhood in Voorhees, New Jersey, in the mid-1990s, the Flyers were a bigger deal than the Eagles, and while I was a bigger fan of baseball than any other sport, the Phillies were an afterthought. So to keep up, I got interested. I asked for a pair of roller blades for my birthday and learned to skate and shoot on my development's long, straight roads, spending my elementary and middle school years playing hockey with the same group of neighborhood kids in a running game that wouldn't need too much editorial massaging to mimic the script of *The Sandlot*.

And Eric Lindros was our Babe Ruth.

By the time I came to Flyers fandom, Lindros was already there, a six-foot four-inch 240-pound native of London, Ontario, who just existed at the center of the Flyers' first line. It didn't occur to me that every team didn't have a player that big, that fast, that skilled, and that tough, that every team's captain didn't merit national media attention and live under such a strict microscope. While I realized that Wayne Gretzky and Mario Lemieux were somehow elevated above the pack,

I thought Mark Messier and Jaromir Jagr and Sergei Fedorov and the other superstar forwards of the time were just the same. It wasn't until years later that I realized that while so many of Lindros's contemporaries went on to greater glory, that wasn't always supposed to be the case.

"He could score 50 goals, get 250 PIMs, get 20 fights on his dance card and win the Hart Trophy—that was the expectation for Eric Lindros," said Jeff Marek of Rogers Sports Net in Canada.

Eric Lindros was born on February 28, 1973, in London, Ontario. His parents, Carl and Bonnie, took an active role in his career from the start—when the Sault Ste. Marie Greyhounds acquired the junior rights to Lindros, his parents engineered a trade closer to their home in London. Lindros was traded to the Oshawa Generals, where he became the OHL's biggest star and won the Memorial Cup, the Canadian major junior national championship.

Lindros brought an unprecedented combination of size, physicality, speed, skill, and toughness to the game—he was supposed to be change-the-rules good, like Wilt Chamberlain or Babe Ruth, and unlike most players in his position, he knew it.

This brings up the bizarre circumstances that brought him to the Flyers.

Lindros was first overall in the 1991 NHL draft to the Quebec Nordiques, a team in one of the league's more remote and smallest markets, and the only wholly French-speaking city with an NHL team, and a team whose owner, Marcel Aubut, was looking to sell the team. Lindros and his parents famously refused to sign with the Nordiques, and Lindros instead held out for the entire 1991–92 season, opting to play junior and international hockey instead of going pro, and deciding to try his luck in the draft again the next year.

This caused a massive stir—Lindros was, apart from Sidney Crosby, the most celebrated draft prospect in recent NHL history, and in hockey-crazed Canada, his holdout shook the sport.

In the meantime, Lindros kept busy. In the summer of 1991, he played for his home country in the Canada Cup, a best-on-best tournament in the days before NHL players went to the Olympics, and won it. Lindros was the only North American player there who wasn't in the NHL. That winter, he played on Team Canada at the World Junior Championships in Germany, where Canada failed to defend the two titles it had won with Lindros in 1990 and 1991, despite 10 points and 12 penalty minutes from Lindros in seven games. Lindros did win a silver medal in the Winter Olympics that year.

Meanwhile, both Lindros and the Nordiques were getting beaten up over the holdout, with Lindros being painted as anti-Francophone and Aubut coming under pressure to make a trade so the NHL would have its most marketable new star in a generation.

"If he would have signed with the Nordiques," Marek said, "that asset would've probably put $60 million in Marcel Aubut's pocket. Eric Lindros knew that, and wanted to be compensated in some way and didn't want to be a key piece of a sale. He's been miscast as someone who hated Quebec and hated the French—he married a Quebec girl, and they've got a baby on the way. There's nothing anti-Francophone about Eric Lindros. He just didn't want to help Marcel Aubut put $60 million in his jeans and then end up in Denver . . . without being compensated."

Eventually, on the eve of the 1992 draft, Aubut gave in and the Nordiques traded Lindros to the Flyers. Or the Rangers.

The Nordiques agreed to trades with both the Flyers and Rangers, and in the confusion, both were reported to the NHL and the press. Flyers owner Ed Snider took the case to arbitration and won. Arbitrator Larry Bertuzzi later told NHL.com: "I was making it up as I went along. And I had no one to consult. And it was highly secretive and it was both the most challenging thing I ever did and one of the loneliest legal things I ever did."

The Flyers got Lindros in exchange for a staggering package: Ron Hextall, Peter Forsberg, Chris Simon, Mike Ricci, Kerry Huffman, Steve Duchesne, two first-round picks, and $15 million. The Rangers' offer was equally preposterous: Doug Weight, Tony Amonte, John Vanbiesbrouck, Alexei Kovalev, three first-rounders and $12 million.

That trade, in addition to bringing Lindros to one of the NHL's richest teams, had two other effects: first, it set up the Nordiques to become, after moving to Colorado in 1995, a perennial Stanley Cup contender. Second, it painted Lindros as a crybaby who didn't know his place in the NHL hierarchy, and his mother and father as meddling stage parents.

"Eric, through his father, Carl, and his mother, Bonnie, and their lawyer, Gord Kirk, understood who Eric was, what he represented, and how much value he brought to the franchise, and they wanted to be compensated as such," Marek said, "which flies in the face of what everyone has always believed about hockey players: they're humble, they put their head down, they say 'Aw, shucks' a lot, they're nice, they're polite—not that Eric wasn't—and they do what they're told. And Eric didn't."

When Lindros returned to Quebec, fans threw pacifiers on the ice. In Philadelphia, however, he was an instant sensation.

As a 19-year-old rookie, Lindros scored 41 goals and recorded 147 penalty minutes in 61 games to finish ninth in Hart Trophy voting and fourth in Calder Trophy voting in a rookie class that included Teemu Selanne's record-setting 76-goal campaign and Joe Juneau's torrid 70-assist campaign. The next year, Lindros scored 44 goals and dished out 53 assists, though the Flyers again missed the playoffs. That offseason, just before the lockout, the Flyers named Lindros team captain, replacing veteran winger Kevin Dineen, and when the season got back underway, they made the second revolutionary trade in three years.

Lindros had been playing on a line with wingers Brent Fedyk and Mark Recchi, the "Crazy Eights" line, for their uniform numbers—Lindros wore No. 88, Fedyk No. 18 and Recchi No. 8. In 1995, they broke up that unit. Recchi, who was the team's leading scorer and a legendary Flyer in his own right, went to the Montreal Canadiens with a third-round pick for Eric Desjardins, John LeClair, and Gilbert Dionne. Desjardins anchored the Flyers' defensive corps, while LeClair, who had been a bit player for a Stanley Cup-winning Montreal squad two years earlier, moved to Lindros' wing, where he became the Kareem to Lindros' Magic. Together with right winger Mikael Renberg, they became known as the Legion of Doom.

In a lockout-shortened 1995 season, Lindros tied for the NHL lead in points, with 70 in 46 games, though he lost the scoring title to Jagr on a tiebreaker. He did win his first and only Hart Trophy and the Flyers, having been absent from the playoffs since 1989, won the division and made it to the Eastern Conference Finals, where they lost to the eventual champion Devils.

1995–96 was Lindros's best year with the Flyers: 47 goals, 68 assists, 115 points, and 163 penalty minutes. The Flyers won another division title, and while they lost in the second round, their core was growing together: Lindros, Renberg, LeClair, Desjardins, and second-line center Rod Brind'Amour were all 26 or younger that year, and they were some good goaltending and a few lucky bounces from winning it all, it seemed.

In 1996–97, the Flyers finally seemed to put it all together: the team brought in veteran defenseman Paul Coffey and rookie Janne Niinimaa to help Desjardins on the blueline and the Flyers tore through the first three rounds of the playoffs like the Kool-Aid man through sheetrock, dispatching Gretzky, Messier, and the New York Rangers in the conference finals. Lindros wound up with 26 points in 19 playoff games and was expected to hoist Philadelphia's first Stanley Cup in 22 years.

"That Philadelphia Flyers team, in my estimation, is probably the best team that never won a Stanley Cup," Marek said. "That year, under Terry Murray, everyone expected them to blast through the Red Wings, *just blast* through them with the Legion of Doom—the Wings shouldn't even have been in the conversation."

That didn't happen. In their first two games at home the Flyers didn't even hold a lead, and things got much worse in Detroit. The Flyers lost in four straight games and got out-scored 16-6 in the process. Snider and GM Bob Clarke kept most of the core: Lindros, LeClair, Desjardins, Brind'Amour, and Hextall, but blew up the rest of the team.

"The problem with the Philadelphia Flyers was, when you lose like that, one of two things can happen: you can to-tally disintegrate or you can learn something," Marek said. "I thought when I was watching that series that as much as this sucks for Philadelphia, the silver lining is that if they learn something from it, they could be a dynasty in the making."

That dynasty was never made. Murray was fired and replaced by assistant coach Wayne Cashman, who was him-self fired after 61 games and replaced by Roger Neilson. Renberg was traded to Tampa Bay for a package including center Chris Gratton, part of a revolving door of support-ing characters. Hextall and Garth Snow shared time with a cavalcade of aging goalies, first Sean Burke in 1997–98. The next summer, Clarke passed on the chance to sign Curtis Jo-seph, the class of the free agent market, to sign 35-year-old John Vanbiesbrouck.

Keith Jones took Renberg's spot on the top line, and while Lindros continued to produce more than a point per game, in-juries began to take their toll and Lindros's relationship with Clarke began to sour.

Clarke was named GM of Team Canada for the 1998 Olympics and not only chose Lindros for the team, but also made him captain, despite Lindros being the second-youngest player on the team—behind Chris Pronger—and despite the presence of certain other legendary captains on the team: Gretzky, Joe Sakic, Ray Bourque, Steve Yzerman, Brendan Shanahan, and Trevor Linden.

Despite the presence of those players, Canada finished out of the medals. After the season, contract negotiations between Clarke and Lindros—or more accurately, Lindros's father, Carl, who was serving as his son's agent—broke down. Then things got worse.

You'll notice that until this point I've been giving Lindros' stats along with the number of games he played in every season. Injuries had always been part and parcel of Lindros' game— it was an outgrowth of the physicality he brought to the ice, as well as a perfect storm of other factors. Perhaps genetics: Lindros' younger brother Brett was the ninth overall draft pick in 1994, but he played only 51 games with the New York Islanders before injuries forced him to retire. He played his last NHL game the week before he turned 20. There's the fact that anything as big as Lindros that moved as quickly as Lindros did carries a tremendous amount of kinetic energy, and when that large, fast-moving thing hits a wall or another player, it takes a beating. There's the fact that even in the late 1990s, sports medicine wasn't as advanced as it is now, and even though hockey is still very much a rub-some-dirt-on-it culture, Lindros might have been treated more carefully by team doctors. And there's probably some bad luck mixed in there too.

Eric Lindros *(AP Photo/Don Heupel)*

But in 1998, the injuries started to get scary. Lindros had the habit of skating with his head down, and as the NHL hadn't had its concussion awakening at that time, players who skated with their heads down were easy targets for the likes of Penguins defenseman Darius Kasparitus, who gave Lindros the first reported concussion of his NHL career. Nine months later, Lindros was hit twice on the same shift in Calgary and gave a quote that would give a modern NHL fan goosebumps: "Helluva shift, eh? I've had better days. It's not anything as bad as what I have had before. It's a bottom-level concussion. I'm not going to miss 19 or 20 games," Lindros said. "Don't make a big deal out of this injury. It's not a big thing . . . We've got games to win."

The next major injury Lindros suffered was the scariest of his career. On April 1, 1999, Lindros was cross-checked during the first period of a game in Nashville. The hit broke a rib, which punctured Lindros' lung and caused three pints of blood to spill into Lindros's chest cavity. Jones, his roommate on the road, convinced Lindros to go to the hospital instead of boarding the team's flight home, a decision that may have saved his life. Lindros and his father criticized the Flyers' training staff for not picking up on the injury before it became life-threatening.

When Lindros returned, he adopted a newly cautious attitude toward his own health. He suffered his next concussion on January 14, 2000, then another on March 4. Team doctors diagnosed the second concussion as a migraine, while Lindros dropped the following bomb to the press:

"The last time I had a concussion, I didn't talk to [Clarke] for three weeks. Then he said off the record that my agent was a fool and disruptive for insisting the team follow return-to-play guidelines."

An infuriated Clarke stripped Lindros of the captaincy and handed it to Desjardins, while Lindros suffered another concussion in May during his rehab, and was only able to play in two postseason games.

The Flyers team to which Lindros returned in late spring of 2000 bore only a passing resemblance to the one he'd led to the Stanley Cup Final in 1997. Though Renberg had returned, Hextall had retired, Niinimaa had been traded for Dan McGillis, and Brind'Amour had been shipped off to Carolina for Keith Primeau. The Flyers had also reacquired Recchi for Dainius Zubrus, who, along with Niinimaa, was the star rookie of the 1997 team, along with draft picks.

The hallmark of that 2000 team was a quartet of rookies: forward Simon Gagne, defensemen Mark Eaton and Andy

Delmore, and goalie Brian Boucher. While Gagne finished fourth on the team in goals, Boucher wrested the starting job away from Vanbiesbrouck and provided the Flyers with the best playoff goaltending they'd had in a decade. Boucher recorded a memorable shutout streak in a tense conference semifinal against Pittsburgh, then took the Flyers to within a game of the Stanley Cup Final against the New Jersey Devils.

The Devils still had several of the key players from their Cup-winning team in 1995: Scott Stevens, Martin Brodeur, Scott Niedermayer, Claude Lemieux, and Ken Daneyko. (Lemieux, the infamous pest, delivered one of my favorite taunts during that series: before a game, he skated up to Desjardins and asked if the C on his jersey stood for "Selfish.") They'd also traded for Alexander Mogilny, one of the best pure goalscorers of his generation.

The Devils also boasted a quartet of impressive rookies: Scott Gomez, Brian Rafalski, Colin White, and John Madden. Between Gomez, Rafalski, Gagne, and Boucher, that series featured 2/3 of the 2000 NHL All-Rookie team.

With the Flyers up 3-1, they failed to win the series at home in Game 5. In Game 6, Lindros, denuded of his trademark C, returned to the lineup, and while he scored the Flyers' only goal, it came in the closing seconds of a game the Flyers were already losing 2-0.

The series returned to Philadelphia two days later, and on his fourth shift of the night and the game still scoreless, Lindros suffered his final concussion as a Flyer. Stevens caught Lindros on the rush with his head down and knocked the Flyers' franchise center out cold. The Flyers, already sputtering offensively, never recovered, and Patrik Elias potted the series winner in the third period. The Flyers wouldn't come that close to winning a Cup for a decade, and Lindros never played for the Flyers again.

Lindros sat out the 2000–01 season to recover, though the drama continued between his family and Clarke, and the rhetoric turned from contentious to vitriolic. (My personal favorite, from Clarke: "I see Eric Desjardins get his teeth knocked out. I didn't hear from his mom and dad. John Le-Clair gets his face torn up with 40 stitches, and we didn't hear from his mom and dad. I'm just so tired of our organization getting beat up so badly by all the accusations the family makes. I don't dislike Eric. I pity him. I feel sorry for him. What's it like to be 27 years old and have your mom and dad running your life? Can't even go to the . . . doctor on your own without your mom and dad coming along.")

On August 20, 2001, Clarke finally traded the rights to Lindros, who was by then a restricted free agent, to the New York Rangers, the team that had narrowly missed out on him a decade earlier.

The package the Flyers got back—Pavel Brendl, Jan Hlavac, Kim Johnsson, and a future third-rounder—paled in comparison to the one they'd given up to get him in 1991.

The rest of Lindros's career wasn't entirely an afterthought—he'd score 73 points in 72 games with the Rangers in 2001–02, plus another goal in the Olympics en route to a gold medal. In 2002–03, he played 81 games, though for the first time in his career, Lindros dipped below a point per game, injuries having not only sapped his body, but also changed the human wrecking ball mentality that made him one of the best players in the league.

"I think he started down the road of injuries . . . at the 1991 Canada Cup, where Mike Keenan used him as a 19-year-old battering ram," Marek said. "It's almost as if he told Eric not even to take his stick out on the ice, because every time Eric was on the ice, he tried to destroy everything in his path. He was big, but he was only 19 years old. It seemed as if that kind of physicality at such a young age really set Eric up for what happened later on in his career."

As Lindros's career wore on—he'd play until the 2004–05 lockout with New York, then enjoy brief stints with the Maple Leafs and Stars thereafter, and we began to learn more about the potential compounding and lasting effects of concussions, that image came to define him. Lindros struggled with injuries of all sorts during his career, but the NHL, at the height of its popularity, watched brain injuries put its biggest star securely in the decline phase of his career at 26 and essentially finish his career by age 30.

"He was the first major league high-profile player where we all stood and watched and waited for the last hit," Marek said.

That fear of the last hit was the reason that I made peace with Lindros leaving the Flyers after such a heartbreaking loss, and with so much business unfinished. As Lindros fans, we didn't act like it at the time, but we knew then that any moment, another opportunistic defenseman might catch Lindros with his head down and not only end his career, but also significantly impact the rest of his life.

Lindros, who retired after the 2007 season at the age of 34, seems to have been quite fortunate in that regard. In a 2013 interview with *ESPN: The Magazine*, Lindros said he feels no adverse effects from his concussions, a sharp contrast to Primeau, who struggles with brain damage from his NHL career to this day. Lindros even buried the hatchet with Clarke and returned to Philadelphia to skate in a Flyers jersey one last time at the Winter Classic Alumni game in 2011, sharing the ice not only with Clarke himself, but also with former linemates LeClair and Recchi. Clarke is now one of Lindros's biggest advocates for induction to the Hall of Fame.

That Lindros only played 760 games in the NHL, only won one MVP, and never won the Stanley Cup makes him a disappointment to some. Even so, he was the best player in the best era of Flyers hockey since the 1970s and he was a martyr in the battle to make hockey safer and less barbaric than it was even in the 1990s. But my greatest disappointment is not that Lindros didn't achieve more. It's rooted in the flashes I get watching Alex Ovechkin's combination of speed, size, and goalscoring ability or David Backes's human cannonball act and deft two-way game, or Wayne Simmonds's aggressiveness and long skating stride. It's the disappointment that nobody's put all that together into one package since Lindros, and I didn't appreciate him enough when I had the chance.

BILL BARBER

7 Bill Barber was one of the Philadelphia area's most successful foreign imports, a hockey player from central Ontario who turned into a Flyers icon and a 30-year fixture in the organization that he took to from his first day as a pro.

Most of Philadelphia's iconic teams developed the dynamic of having one memorable player on offense and defense: White and Cunningham, Dawkins and McNabb, Roberts and Ashburn, Carlton and Schmidt, and Parent and Clarke. As he was neither the captain and MVP of the Broad Street Bullies, nor the Vezina Trophy-winning goalie, Barber often gets forgotten. Though Barber is the Flyers' all-time leading goalscorer, there's no one iconic image or facet of the game that suits him. And he's fine with that.

"I tried to play an all-around game," Barber said. "That's what I took the most pride in. To be consistent, I guess, would be the one word that I wanted to be remembered as, as a player who was there game in and game out."

Barber came into the NHL as a hot prospect, the anchor of a line for the Kitchener Rangers that produced three first-round draft picks, including Barber, and he was very cognizant of his chances of making a career as a hockey player.

"I knew I could play," Barber said. "Even before I turned pro, I knew I could play. Being in Kitchener, the three years I spent there . . . the New York Rangers would have their training camp there. Every so often a line would drop down and play with us, and we could play with them. The line I played on with Al Blanchard and Jerry Byers, we could hold our own. Even though we were in our last year of junior, we could go head-to-head with an NHL line."

Barber scored 298 points in 177 OHL games and went seventh overall in the 1972 draft to the Flyers, a relatively new expansion team. It might seem crazy to say this nearly 50 years after, but in 1967, when the NHL expanded from six teams to 12, Philadelphia was a somewhat risky expansion into the American South. Barber was happy to come to the South for both historic and more pragmatic reasons: twice as many teams meant twice as many NHL jobs.

"I loved the thought process of expansion, period," Barber said, "because as a young player it gives you a better opportunity to make it to the NHL and play."

In 1971–72, the NHL had 14 teams in two divisions of seven teams each, and the East Division featured five of the more established Original Six teams. The Flyers managed to miss the playoffs that year despite playing in the weaker West Division, which Barber viewed as a positive.

"I remember Montreal having the fourth, sixth, and eighth picks in the first round," Barber said. "I was kind of rated in around an area there, and I went seventh to Philadelphia. I was very, very happy—no disrespect to Montreal, but it gave me a chance to go to an expansion team that hopefully would better my odds of making it."

As concerned as Barber says he was about sticking with the NHL, he quickly proved to everyone that he belonged. Barber scored 14 points in 11 games for the Richmond Robins, then found himself in Philadelphia with the big club, where he made an immediate mark with 64 points in 69 games to finish a close second in voting for the NHL's rookie of the year award, the Calder Trophy.

Barber was one of the last pieces to fall into place on the Broad Street Bullies teams that won back-to-back Stanley Cups, and he fit in immediately with two of the team's most important figures: captain Bobby Clarke and head coach Fred Shero.

The narrative surrounding those Flyers teams today is that they gooned their way to the title. However, Shero was a revolutionary figure in North American hockey coaching, becoming the first NHL coach to replace the traditional Canadian dump-and-chase style with the European possession game.

"That wasn't Fred Shero's system," said Jeff Marek of Rogers Sports Net. "That was the Anatoli Tarasov Soviet system. The one coach who could check his ego at the door and say, 'I want to learn something from Soviet hockey. I want to learn something from European hockey' was Fred Shero."

Barber, an extremely intelligent, well-rounded player, fit perfectly in a style that called for players to constantly be on the move and on the lookout for the puck. Barber, who had played center in junior, played all over for Shero, moving to Clarke's wing and playing the point on the power play with Tom Bladon.

Moving to Shero's system could have been a difficult adjustment for a 20-year-old rookie, but Barber came prepared. His brother had played for Shero in the minor leagues and gave Bill advance warning.

"He made mention to me about the fact that if you can't play for Fred Shero, you can't play," Barber said. "It was about as simple as that. He was a unique man that gave all young players the opportunity to play. [Shero] gave me the opportunity to play and then assume responsibilities on the team as far as power play and penalty killing."

Shero made young players the centerpiece of his Flyers team, perhaps because he had no choice—young players were what he had. But they took to Shero's system and improved rapidly. In Barber's rookie year, the Flyers improved by 19 points. The next season, the Flyers reacquired Bernie Parent and improved by another 27 points, and on Clarke's wing, the 21-year-old Barber turned into a weapon.

"When [Fred Shero] put Bill Barber on the wing with Bobby Clarke, it was magical," Marek said. "Bill Barber could fill the net—he was money in the bank when he got the puck on his stick, but he was a complete hockey player. He could do whatever Fred Shero asked—he wasn't that one-dimensional hockey player."

Clarke, Rick MacLeish, and Barber finished 1-2-3 on the Flyers in points and combined to score 101 of the team's 273 goals between the three of them, then kept up the heat in the playoffs as MacLeish scored 13 more in 17 games en route to the Flyers' first title.

The next year, the Flyers brought in another weapon, California Golden Seals winger Reggie Leach, who partnered with Barber and Clarke to form the now-famous LCB line. The three combined for 104 goals—and Clarke chipped in a staggering 89 assists—and the Flyers, following the NHL's expansion and realignment into four divisions, cakewalked to win the Patrick Division by 25 points. Barber chipped in 15 more points in the playoffs as the Flyers won their second straight Stanley Cup.

In 1975–76, the Flyers were even better, despite Parent's absence, as the LCB line turned in its best performance. Clarke won the Hart Trophy with a 119-point performance, while Barber contributed a career-high 50 goals and 112 points and Leach scored a franchise record 61 goals.

In the playoffs, the Flyers beat the Maple Leafs 4-3 and breezed past the Bruins to set up a confrontation with the Montreal Canadiens in the Stanley Cup Final.

The 1975–76 Flyers might have been the best team in franchise history—Barber said it was the most talented of the Broad Street Bullies teams—but the Canadiens were even better. Coached by Scotty Bowman, the Canadiens boasted Vezina Trophy winner Ken Dryden in net, NHL leading scorer Guy Lafleur up front, and seven other Hall of Famers in between. Leach became the first skater to win the Conn Smythe in a losing effort, but the Canadiens won four straight close games to end the Flyers' chances at a three-peat.

"We played a lot of hockey in that three-year period," Barber said. "We had a lot of guys banged up, so maybe that fatigue factor was there."

Even though Barber was only 23 during the 1975–76 season, he had already reached his greatest individual heights as a player, and following two consecutive playoff losses to Boston in 1977 and 1978, Shero left Philadelphia to coach the New York Rangers. In 1978–79, the Flyers struggled at first under new coach Bob McCammon before Pat Quinn came in to straighten things out. In 1979–80, the Flyers returned to the Stanley Cup Final with part of the core from the mid-1970s. Parent had retired by then, and Clarke and MacLeish, now in their 30s, gave up part of the load. Barber himself began another positional transition, playing defense in certain situations, especially 4-on-4, as two new young forwards, Ken Linseman, 21, and Brian Propp, 20, posted 79 and 75 points, respectively. Winger Paul Holmgren, 24, chipped in 65 points and 267 penalty minutes, and 22-year-old Pete Peeters took over the lion's share of the goaltending duties. Twenty-four-year-old Mel Bridgman, who had taken over the captaincy to allow Clarke to become a player-coach, contributed 47 points of his own. Thanks to Quinn's leadership, the influx of new young forward depth, and the remaining core of veterans, the Flyers reeled off an NHL-record 35-game unbeaten streak and went on to face the New York Islanders in the Stanley Cup Final.

Barber chipped in 21 points in the playoffs, a career high. Those points went wasted, however, when the Islanders won Game 6 in overtime, thanks in part to a famous blown offside call on a Duane Sutter goal.

Bill Barber *(AP Photo)*

The next season, Barber led the Flyers in scoring for the first time in his career, with 43 goals and 85 points, then followed it up with his third straight 40-goal season in 1981–82, a disappointing season that included the Flyers trading Bridgman, firing Quinn in favor of McCammon, and then going out in the first round to the Rangers.

With Bridgman gone, Barber assumed the captaincy in 1982, and while the Flyers rebounded to first place, Barber himself was suffering the results of years of injuries.

"My last couple years I wasn't overly pleased with," Barber said. "I wasn't on top of my game—that knee problem was always nipping at me. I had a serious knee injury in 1974–75, and I got the years out of it that I did. The last few years as a player were not years that I'd say that were the best I could do."

Barber retired after the 1983–84 season at age thirty-one, and he and Clarke, who retired the same year, went into the Flyers' front office together. Barber developed an affinity for working with younger players and spent the next decade in scouting and player development, including filling in as coach of the Flyers' farm team, the Hershey Bears, for 16 games in 1984–85.

With the Flyers having moved into the building now known as the Wells Fargo Center, the organization opted to start a new minor league club across the street in the old Spectrum, where Clarke and Barber had won their Stanley Cups. Having paid his dues in the front office, Barber asked his old friend if he could coach the newly-minted Phantoms.

"I came up from Hershey and went to Clarkie and said, 'Can I see you for a minute?' I was living in Hershey at the time, and I went down right after Christmas that year. I said, 'What are you going to be doing coaching-wise when you bring the minor league team here, to Philly?'

"He says, 'Do you want a job?'

"And I said, 'Yeah, I'll take it.'"

Barber was an immediate success, winning the Mid-Atlantic Division title in each of his first three seasons behind the bench and taking home the Calder Cup, the AHL's championship trophy, in 1997–98. After four years in the minors, Barber got his break as a coach. Clarke, who had developed a short leash with coaches, fired Craig Ramsay after a 12-12-4 start in 2000–01, and promoted Barber, who went 31-13-7-3 in 54 games and salvaged a playoff appearance, winning the Jack Adams Award as the NHL's coach of the year in his first season. Barber followed that up with a division title in 2001–02, but his playoff performance was found wanting. Barber's Flyers were knocked out in the first round twice in as many chances, the second a humiliating 4-1 defeat to Ottawa in which the Flyers scored one regulation goal in the entire series. After the 2002 playoffs, Clarke replaced Barber with Ken Hitchcock.

Barber hasn't coached since, though he looks back at the experience fondly and as an extension of his playing partnership with Clarke.

"It was good," he said. "I thank Clarkie first of all for giving me the opportunity to do that, and for giving me the opportunity prior to that to coach the minor league team, to gain the experience, so I welcomed the opportunity to go do that. I wish we could've done better—we fell a little bit short, but it was a great experience for me to be part of the organization, which I was for 30 years."

Barber went on to serve as director of player personnel for the Tampa Bay Lightning for six years, but he's currently part of a large contingent of ex-Flyers who, instead of returning to Canada after retiring, remained in the Delaware Valley.

"If you look at the amount of ex-players, alumni, who are around the area, it's unbelievable," Barber said. "I think what it is, is that when you have success, people welcome that. They love to see you play and you just get warm to the area. You meet a lot of good people outside of hockey, you meet a lot of good people in the business end of things and you just don't want to leave."

Barber was attracted to Philadelphia as a young player because he thought it would be easier to make his name in an expansion city. What he found after 30 years in the Flyers organization was that the expansion city he'd showed up in as a 20-year-old would go on to make him.

"I came up at the right time, got involved with the right organization, the right teammates, and all that," Barber said. "I'm very fortunate and still grateful to this day that I had the teammates that I had and the ownership that we had with Mr. Snider and Keith Allen being our general manager and Fred Shero being our coach."

The organization, it seems, agreed. Barber was part of the second class of the Flyers' Hall of Fame in 1989, along with Allen and Snider, and was inducted to the Phantoms Hall of Fame in 2005. In 1990, Barber was inducted to the Hockey Hall of Fame, and that October, the Flyers retired his No. 7 jersey.

ROBIN ROBERTS

8 It's hard to believe how little drama surrounds the career of Robin Roberts. As great as he was, there isn't a moment or quote that defines him, nor a physical feature or photograph. A modern-day Phillies fan probably knows a few things about Roberts: that he was a pitcher, and a good one. He wore No. 36, because the Phillies retired it, and he was the best pitcher on the Whiz Kids of 1950. All anyone seems to say about Roberts as a person is that he was just a nice guy—Philadelphia broadcaster Bill Campbell once called Roberts the classiest athlete in Philadelphia history, for whatever that's worth. But among great Phillies pitchers, Roberts remains something of a blank slate.

Roberts didn't have Steve Carlton's wipeout slider, stack of individual awards and records, and contentious relationship with the media. He didn't throw with Cliff Lee's pinpoint control or magnetic self-confidence. He didn't have a devastating signature changeup or look like he'd just stepped off the set of a *Twilight* movie, like Cole Hamels does. He didn't pout or shoot off his mouth, like Curt Schilling, when things went bad. He was just an average-looking guy who relentlessly threw strikes, recorded outs, and won baseball games for a team that, in 13 of his 14 seasons in Philadelphia, didn't get or deserve much in the way of national press coverage.

Roberts didn't win 300 games, strike out 3,000 batters, or win a World Series, but his career was immensely impressive, even if there's no simple reason why.

Robin Roberts was born to Welsh immigrants in Springfield, Illinois, on September 26, 1926. His military service during World War II took him to East Lansing, Michigan, where he returned after the war to attend Michigan State. Though he lettered three times for the basketball team, Roberts never dreamed of playing professional sports growing up.

"There was no television back then," Roberts said in a 2002 appearance at Michigan State. "We'd follow the major leagues through the radio and we knew who all the players were. I didn't give any thought to being a professional athlete. The guys in the big leagues were bigger than life. You couldn't associate yourself with them. I thought I'd be a teacher and coach."

Nevertheless, he approached Spartan baseball coach John Kobs after his sophomore year and tried out. Having no preference on what position he played, Roberts made the team as a pitcher for no other reason than because Kobs told him that's what the team needed.

For the next year, Roberts played basketball in the winter and baseball in the spring and summer (pitching for the Spartans in the spring, then playing summer ball in Vermont when school let out). Before the 1948 season, the Philadelphia Phillies signed him to a $10,000 contract and assigned the 21-year-old Roberts to Class-B Wilmington, where he needed only 11 games to convince the club he was ready for the majors. Once there, he needed almost no time to adjust.

Roberts allowed two runs on five hits in eight innings in his major league debut, a 2-0 loss to the Pirates on June 18, 1948, and completed seven of his next eight starts, winning six.

In 1949, Roberts began a 12-year streak in which he made at least 30 starts and completed 10 every year, and in 1950, he enjoyed his most famous season, if not necessarily his best. At age 23, Roberts led the National League in starts and shutouts, threw more than 300 innings for the first time, and won 20 games for the first time. He made his first of seven straight All-Star teams and the Phillies won their first pennant in 35 years as Roberts, along with fellow youngsters Bubba Church and Curt Simmons, as well as relief ace and National League MVP Jim Konstanty, helped the Phillies' staff become the best in the National League. Roberts not only led the team in innings pitched by nearly 100, but he also got the ball in the last game of the year, with the season on the line, only three days after pitching a combined 12 innings in both ends of a doubleheader.

Roberts faced Dodgers ace Don Newcombe—and if you wanted to see one game in the early 1950s, with the National League pennant on the line, Newcombe vs. Roberts is probably the pitching matchup you'd choose—and Roberts, who had lost his previous three decisions, matched Newcombe blow for blow, going 10 innings and allowing one run, though he needed a little bit of ninth-inning defensive help to keep the Dodgers from winning the game and tying the Phillies in the standings. (See the Richie Ashburn chapter for more on that particular play.) The Phillies won, 4-1, in 10 innings and held on to the pennant.

There's a history of great pitchers using one high-pressure game to announce a Hall of Fame career, to the point where we expect every 23-year-old who throws a shutout in the playoffs to go on to greatness. But that game, and to a larger extent, that season, was Roberts's coming-out party.

Come the World Series, Roberts had been worn down to a blunt nub by overuse and Simmons was on active military duty, so Konstanty made the Game 1 start and lost. Roberts took over in Game 2 and once again found himself on the mound with the Phillies' season in peril and one of the game's best starting pitchers, Allie Reynolds, on the mound for the other team.

Once again, Roberts allowed one run in nine innings and found the teams tied after regulation. This time, however, Joe DiMaggio led off the 10th inning with a solo home run and the Yankees won 2-1.

Two days later, the Phillies, down 3-0 in the series by this point, sent Bob Miller to the mound to salvage the season. After four batters, the Yankees had already beaten two runs out of Miller and Phillies manager Eddie Sawyer had seen enough. He called for Konstanty, who surrendered three more runs over 6 ⅔ innings. Roberts, on one day's rest, pitched one scoreless inning of relief, and while the Phillies got two unearned runs out of Whitey Ford (making *his* World Series debut) to bring the tying run to the plate in the ninth inning, Reynolds came in to face one batter, Stan Lopata, who struck out to end the series. Roberts, 23, never pitched in the World Series again, nor would any Phillies pitcher for another 30 years.

From that point on, Roberts was the best pitcher in baseball, and in most seasons, it wasn't particularly close. He threw more innings than any pitcher in the game, and those innings were better pitched. During his seven-year peak, 1950 to 1956, Roberts threw 2,235 innings, most in baseball by almost 300. During those years, only 24 other pitchers threw even half as many innings. He started the most games (by 26), completed the most games (by 30), recorded the most shutouts, and despite playing for largely terrible teams, won the most games.

Not only did Roberts blow away his competition in terms of quantity, but also he held his own in terms of quality as well. Among pitchers who threw at least 1,000 innings in those seven seasons, Roberts was sixth in adjusted ERA and walked by far the fewest batters on a per-inning basis. Roberts walked 1.59 batters per nine innings—Newcombe and Eddie Lopat tied for second with 2.27. Over the course of his entire career, Roberts walked 1.73 batters per nine innings, seventh among all post-integration starting pitchers with at least 1,000 innings, and one spot better than Greg Maddux.

Throw it all together and Roberts, from 1950–1956, was worth 49.2 wins above replacement. The next three pitchers on the list are Warren Spahn (43 wins), Billy Pierce (33.8), and Early Wynn (32.6). Nobody else reaches 30. Counting Roberts's contributions with the bat and the glove, Baseball Reference rates him as being worth 54.8 wins during his seven-year peak. The only post-integration starters with a better peak: Roger Clemens, Randy Johnson, Bob Gibson, Tom Seaver, Pedro Martinez, and Maddux.

Of course, throwing that many innings can take its toll on a smaller pitcher, and Roberts, who was listed at six feet, 190 pounds, started to develop shoulder problems during the 1956 season. Despite leading the National League in K/BB ratio that year, no National League pitcher allowed more hits, runs, or home runs, and Roberts suffered a career-high 18 losses. His ERA stayed over 4.00 in 1957, though he rebounded for his last great season with the Phillies in 1958, when he went 17-14 with a 3.24 ERA and 6.2 WAR. Roberts's decline continued through the 1961 season, in which he went 1-10 with a 5.85 ERA.

Not even Roberts could survive a season like that, and the Phillies sold the best pitcher in franchise history to the Yankees on October 16, 1961.

Robin Roberts *(AP Photo)*

It was difficult to cut the cord with Roberts, however, and when the Phillies and Yankees played during Spring Training the following year, the Phillies made his No. 36 the first number they retired. The Phillies haven't retired an active player's number since. Said Roberts of the ceremony: "[E]verybody cried—especially the National League hitters."

Roberts never appeared in a game with the Yankees, who cut him in late May. The same day, Roberts caught on with the Orioles and spent three and a half largely successful seasons in Baltimore. After Roberts developed shoulder problems in

1956, he continued to throw in excess of 260 innings a year, but perhaps pitching only half a season in 1961—he was on the roster pretty much all year, but only threw 117 innings and faced 512 batters—allowed Roberts to recover somewhat.

At any rate, Roberts's rate statistics with the Orioles were similar to his numbers with the Phillies—115 ERA+, 2.61 K/BB ratio, 4.8 K/9 with Baltimore, compared to a 114 ERA+, 2.60 K/BB ratio and 4.7 K/9 with the Phillies—but in his late 30s, Roberts was no longer pitching the same absurd volume of innings as before.

By mid-1965, the Orioles were assembling the starting rotation that would win them the World Series the next year, plus three pennants in a row under Earl Weaver from 1969–71: 22-year-old Dave McNally, 20-year-old Wally Bunker, and 19-year-old Jim Palmer began to squeeze out the veterans, including Roberts. Roberts, despite not pitching particularly poorly, was out of the rotation by late June and off the team entirely on July 31.

The 38-year-old Roberts, now in bounce-around mode, signed with the Houston Astros and made an immediate impact: his Astros debut was a four-hit complete-game shutout of (as fate would have it) the Phillies, and Roberts followed it up with another four-hit shutout a week later, this one against the Pirates, then a two-run, nine-hit complete-game victory over the Cubs.

Roberts pitched the rest of 1965 and the first half of 1966 with Houston, throwing the last of his 45 career complete game shutouts on May 4. He then finished out his major league career, and after a fruitless comeback attempt with the minor league Reading Phillies the next season, Roberts retired at the age of 40.

It was an impressive career, but Roberts still doesn't get the respect he is due. This is, I believe, due to three factors that have nothing to do with his personality or the quality of his teams.

The first is that despite being one of the hardest-throwing pitchers of his era (Hall of Famer Ralph Kiner said Roberts had the best fastball he ever saw), Roberts didn't strike out a ton of batters—only 2,357 in his career, which is a funny thing to say, *only* 2,357 strikeouts. But Hall of Fame voters and casual fans love round numbers, and Roberts didn't get to 300 wins or 3,000 strikeouts, because he played in an era where batters valued contact over power and didn't strike out as much, and because his teams were terrible. Okay, maybe it has a little to do with the quality of his teams.

But there are two types of extremely hard throwers. The first kind uses the fastball to generate swings and misses, either on its own or as a setup for a breaking ball: Nolan Ryan, Randy Johnson, Sandy Koufax, and so on. The second throws the fastball for strikes almost exclusively, and while Schilling, Clemens, and Seaver threw it down in the zone for ground balls, Roberts would just pump it down the middle to get ahead in the count. Working ahead in the count gives a pitcher options and allows him to record outs using fewer pitches and work deeper into games, to say nothing of not creating unnecessary baserunners through walks. Among current pitchers, Nationals righthander Jordan Zimmermann is most like this, a pitcher who throws extremely hard, doesn't strike out a ton of guys, and gets away with it.

The flip side is that pitchers who pound the strike zone invite contact, and pitchers who invite contact, even pitchers as good as Roberts, can get beaten up a little. Roberts led the National League in hits allowed five times, all during that insane 1950–56 streak, and famously held the record for home runs allowed until Jamie Moyer passed him in 2010.

Roberts pitched almost impatiently, working quickly and pounding the strike zone, with a distaste for hitters who tried to work the count. This style probably cost him strikeouts compared to contemporaries who skirted the zone or tried to get hitters to chase, and because Roberts wasn't afraid of giving up contact, he allowed more hits than his contemporaries, including, say, Sandy Koufax.

In fact, Roberts's approach to pitching was almost absurdly simple. He told *Time* magazine in July 1956:

> "You don't have to make a big study of batters beforehand. When I have good stuff I throw four fastballs out of five pitches. When you take up a hitter in a clubhouse meeting, no matter what his weakness is, it's going to end up low and away or high and tight, and the curveball must be thrown below the belt. That's the whole story of pitching. Keep your life and your pitching real simple and you'll get along."

The second reason Roberts is undervalued is that what we consider important for a pitcher today was not as important when he pitched. Roberts's tremendous command and control didn't go unnoticed, but walks weren't considered an offensive weapon in the 1950s the way they are today, so Roberts's ability to prevent them wasn't as lauded as it would be today (you're welcome, Cliff Lee). Wins were also more important as a method of evaluation, which hurts pitchers who play for teams that lose 90 games a year, as Roberts did. Today, we'd be far more impressed with his innings total than his wins total.

In addition, the public baseball debate hadn't developed to the point it has today, and a player's legacy largely came down to counting stats over the course of a career. Roberts pitched long enough to rack up impressive counting numbers, but Hall of Fame voters and sportswriters of the 1960s and 1970s weren't separating out peak performance the way they do now, and using it as a career evaluator. Therefore, players like Roberts, who got beat up in their hangaround phase, get punished in their career rate totals, compared to players, again, like Koufax, who hung it up before they started to decline.

The third reason Roberts is so underrated is actually an interesting theory set forth by Bill James: they started giving out the Cy Young about five years too late.

As I mentioned above, Roberts, from 1950–56, was far and away the best pitcher in baseball, but at the time, we had no award to commemorate it. The Cy Young was first given out in 1956, which is the year Roberts's peak ended. According to James's Win Shares system, Roberts was the best pitcher in the

National League in every year from 1950–55, except for 1951, when he finished in a practical dead heat with Sal Maglie. If the Cy Young existed then as it does now, Roberts would have won at least one and perhaps as many as four. Greg Maddux's reputation is built in part from having won the Cy Young four years in a row—if Roberts had done that, he'd be absolutely legendary, because his peak was pretty much as good as Maddux's.

Unlike his teammate Ashburn, Roberts didn't stick around Philadelphia long enough to become an institution. He did color commentary for one year in 1976, then moved to Florida to become head baseball coach at the University of South Florida. As coach of the Bulls, Roberts went 262-240-1, made the NCAA Tournament in 1982, and coached four future major leaguers before retiring for good in 1985.

Roberts, who was one of the early leaders of the Major League Baseball Players Association and a key figure in hiring legendary union boss Marvin Miller, remained active throughout his retirement, becoming one of the first vocal critics of pitcher overuse in Little League and serving as a Spring Training instructor for the Phillies. After his retirement, Roberts was routinely named to various historical All-Star teams, including the All-Century Team and James's list of the 100 best players of all time, published in the *New Historical Baseball Abstract* in 2001. Roberts was elected to the Hall of Fame in 1976 and died at his home in Florida in 2010, at the age of eighty-three.

BERNIE PARENT

9 On New Year's Eve, 2011, Bernie Parent put on a Flyers jersey and pads one last time. At 66, he started for the Flyers in an alumni game against the New York Rangers on the eve of the 2012 Winter Classic, and he stopped all five shots he faced, including a breakaway effort from Ron Duguay. A capacity crowd at Citizens Bank Park got into the act, chanting "Bernie! Bernie! Bernie!" as the Flyers' greatest-ever goalie appeared one last time for the fans.

Parent was born on April 3, 1945 in Montreal, the youngest of seven children. He grew up playing street hockey and eventually joined a bantam team that was coached by his oldest brother, Yvan. The younger Parent took to goaltending quickly and idolized Jacques Plante, the legendary Montreal Canadiens goalie, which had a huge impact on Parent's development, even if idolizing Plante wasn't exactly unusual among young French-Canadian goalies.

When it came time to play junior, Parent left his native Quebec for the first time and moved, for the first time, to the Anglophone part of Canada to catch on with the Niagra Falls Flyers, where he led the OHA (the predecessor to the OHL,

Ontario's major junior league) in goals against average twice and took home the Memorial Cup, Canadian junior hockey's national championship, in 1965.

Playing junior in Niagra Falls had two significant impacts on Parent's career: first, it forced him to become comfortable with English, which was a struggle for Parent early in his career. Second, it took him out of the territorial zone of the Montreal Canadiens, leaving him open to sign with the Boston Bruins after his amateur career.

Parent made his debut with the Bruins at age twenty, and he actually led a pretty terrible Boston team in games played and goals against average as a rookie, while finishing fourth in the Calder Trophy voting. Boston scored the fewest goals in the six-team NHL and allowed the most, escaping last place by one point. That Bruins team would become legendary within half a decade, but those pieces hadn't arrived yet: Bobby Orr and Phil Esposito had yet to make their debuts, and Derek Sanderson played only two games as a 19-year-old rookie in 1965–66.

Parent bounced between Boston and the Oklahoma City Blazers the next season as veterans Gerry Cheevers and Eddie Johnston took the reins back. That offseason, the NHL expanded from six teams to twelve, and the Bruins left Parent and another twenty-two-year-old goalie prospect, Doug Favell, unprotected in the expansion draft. One of the league's new teams, the Philadelphia Flyers, snatched up the pair, taking Parent in the first round between fellow Hall of Fame goalies Glenn Hall and Terry Sawchuk.

Parent and Favell, who wore the No. 1 jersey that would eventually become Parent's signature, worked as a tandem for the Flyers's first season, in which Parent went 16-17-5 with a 2.48 GAA and four shutouts and Favell went 15-15-6 with a 2.27 GAA and four shutouts of his own. By the playoffs, Parent had pretty well locked down the starting job, which he held from Favell for the next two and a half seasons, until a February 1, 1971 trade shook up the organization. The Flyers traded Parent and a second-round draft pick to the Toronto Maple Leafs for goalie Bruce Gamble (who would back up Favell for a season and a half after Parent's departure), winger Mike Walton, and a first-round pick. The same day, the Flyers flipped Walton for two more young forwards: Danny Schock and Rick MacLeish.

MacLeish entered the starting lineup full-time in 1972–73, and in his first full NHL season, became the first 50-goal scorer in franchise history. MacLeish went on to become an integral part of the Flyers' two Stanley Cup teams, finishing second on the team in scoring in 1973–74 and 1974–75 and leading both Stanley Cup teams in playoff goals.

Parent, for his part, was left in limbo somewhat, having been demoted from starter in Philadelphia to backup in Toronto, and the trade upset not only Parent, who enjoyed playing in Philadelphia for then-coach Keith Allen, but Philadelphia fans as well.

As backup jobs went at the time, however, Parent's was a special one, as he found himself playing behind the goalie he'd grown up idolizing in Montreal: Jacques Plante. Parent had been a competent starter in Philadelphia, but he often played an uncontrolled style. Plante mentored and helped rein in twenty-five-year-old Parent.

"In 1971, Jacques Plante had a .948 save percentage," said Jeff Marek of Rogers SportsNet and co-host of the Marek vs. Wyshynski podcast. "It's one of the greatest goaltending performances of all time . . . and Bernie Parent was his backup. Bernie learned from Jacques Plante how to become more of an angles goaltender, how to play angles as opposed to being this wild, outrageous [goalie] that he was when he played for the Niagra Falls Flyers of the OHA."

Parent soon eclipsed Plante as the Maple Leafs's starter, making four playoff starts in 1971 and 47 more in the 1971–72 regular season. But when the opportunity to return to Philadelphia came up, Parent jumped at it.

Bernie Parent *(AP Photo/Brian Horton)*

In 1972, the rival World Hockey Association, pro hockey's answer to the flashy ABA, moved a franchise to Philadelphia, and the Philadelphia Blazers immediately took aim at the NHL's Flyers by signing Parent, former Flyer Andre Lacroix, and Parent's old Boston teammate Derek Sanderson, who had by then grown into a star with the Bruins. The results were mixed. Lacroix scored a league-leading 124 points, while Parent played 63 games, second in the league among goalies, but struggled in the more freewheeling WHA, allowing more goals than anyone else in the league. Sanderson, whose five-year, $2.6 million contract made him the highest-paid hockey player in history, played only eight games before returning to Boston and the NHL. The Blazers finished under .500 and were swept out of the playoffs in the first round, then moved to Vancouver the next year, leaving Parent the choice between coming with them or returning to the Maple Leafs. After losing Parent to the WHA over a salary dispute, Leafs owner Harold Ballard offered Parent even less money going into 1973–74, and Parent balked at the offer. After Parent threatened to hold out, Ballard relented and worked out a trade that would send Parent and a second-round pick to the Flyers for a first-rounder and Parent's old backup, Doug Favell.

The Flyers, meanwhile, had been busy in Parent's absence. In addition to MacLeish, the Flyers had acquired Bill Barber, Terry Crisp, Dave Schultz, and head coach Fred Shero, who preached a fluid, fast-moving, Soviet style of hockey that, along with the Flyers' penchant for physical dominance, made them extremely difficult to play against.

And the 28-year-old Parent who came back to the Flyers was an entirely different goalie than the one they'd traded away two and a half years earlier.

"By the time the Philadelphia Flyers won the Stanley Cup in 1974," Marek said, "Bernie Parent was the best angles goaltender in the NHL, maybe the best in the history of the game. Nobody understood angles and that type of positioning [as much as] Bernie Parent. For my money, as much as people talk about Tony Esposito and Ken Dryden, the best goaltender of the '70s, hands down, was Bernie Parent."

In 1973–74, Parent was outstanding: he led the league in games and minutes played by a goalie, as well as wins, shutouts (12), and GAA (1.89), which earned him the Vezina Trophy as the league's top goaltender, as well as a close runner-up to Esposito for the Hart Trophy as league MVP.

Parent was just as good in the playoffs, playing all 1,042 postseason minutes for the Flyers, who made their first Stanley Cup Final. They dropped the first game 3-2 in Boston, putting them behind in a playoff series for the only time all year, then stormed back to win four of the next five, including a 1-0 Parent shutout in Game Six to seal the series and give the Flyers the first Stanley Cup not only in the city's history, but also the first for any expansion team.

Parent more or less replicated his season in 1974–75, again leading the league in wins, GAA, and shutouts and taking home the Vezina. This time, he finished fourth in Hart Trophy voting behind, among others, his teammate Bobby Clarke.

Parent only played 15 of the Flyers' 17 playoff games this time around, but he registered four shutouts, including, again, the Cup clincher, this one a 2-0 win over the Buffalo Sabres, and took home his second straight Conn Smythe Trophy as MVP of the playoffs.

At age twenty-nine and coming off two of the best seasons by any goalie in NHL history, Parent's future looked bright, but he would, in fact, only play 157 more regular-season games from the end of the 1974–75 season to the end of his career. The Flyers made a third run at the Cup in 1975–76, but a preseason neck injury limited Parent to only 11 regular-season games and eight more in the playoffs, where he split time with the more effective Wayne Stephenson en route to the Montreal Canadiens's sweep of the Flyers in the Stanley Cup Finals.

Parent started 61 games in 1976–77, winning 35 and posting a 2.71 GAA, and before the 1977–78 season, the Flyers brought in Plante, Parent's onetime idol and later teammate, to serve as goaltending coach. Plante helped Parent return to form, shave half a goal off his GAA, and lead the league in shutouts for a third and final time. Parent was playing fairly well in 1978–79 before, on Feburary 17, a stray stick hit him in the eye, damaging his vision and ending his career at the age of 33.

Parent is the classic exemplar of peak versus longevity. He played a full healthy season behind a good team maybe four times in his career, and when he did, he was spectacular. Along with Clarke, Parent was the most important member of the Flyers's only two title teams, and while the organization has cycled through Hall of Fame forwards and defensemen over the years, they've had truly elite, veteran, dependable goaltending only a handful of times in franchise history, and they enjoyed their greatest success with their greatest goalie between the pipes.

On October 11, 1979, the Flyers retired Parent's No. 1, making his the second jersey number they retired, after Barry Ashbee, a key defenseman on the first title team who died of leukemia in 1977. Parent was inducted to the Hockey Hall of Fame in 1984, the first Flyer player to be so honored. In 1988, the Flyers opened their own team hall of fame, with Parent and Clarke as charter members.

After his retirement, Parent remained in the organization, first as a scout, then as a goaltending coach, first working alongside Plante and later on his own. In the 1980s, he mentored a young Swedish goalie named Pelle Lindbergh, who had idolized Parent as a boy and had grown up a Flyers fan as a result. Parent became to Lindbergh what Plante had been to him, and under Parent's tutelage, Lindbergh won a Vezina Trophy of his own in 1985, becoming the first European-born goalie to do so. That fall, Lindbergh was killed in a car crash, and Parent, though shaken by his death, went to work on Lindbergh's replacement, Ron Hextall, who won the Vezina and the Conn Smythe two years later.

In total, Flyers goalies have won the Vezina four times and the Conn Smythe three times, and every one of those awards belonged to Parent or a goalie he taught. Since then, the Flyers haven't seen anyone like him.

DONOVAN McNABB

10 This one's tough, because SB Nation's Jon Bois has already written the Donovan McNabb essay that I wanted to write.[3] Bois is—perhaps necessarily if you're going to write about McNabb objectively—not an Eagles fan and not a Philadelphian, South Jerseyite, or Northeasterner of any kind. His piece, titled "Haunted by Stupidity," is a wonderful six-part work of criticism with GIFs and infographics, and if you haven't read it already, you must. It addresses the hostile media and fan culture that haunted McNabb during his 11 seasons with the Eagles, changing McNabb's legacy from "best offensive player in franchise history and beloved icon" to "complainer, choker, disappointment."

Oh, and "persecution complex." If that's true, McNabb is the walking embodiment of Henry Kissinger's famous quote: "Even paranoids have enemies."

In fact, McNabb's inclusion on this list at all will probably shock some of you, who might think that if an Eagles quarterback was going to make this list, it would be Randall Cunningham or Ron Jaworski. Or Norm Van Brocklin or

---

3 http://www.sbnation.com/nfl/2013/8/21/4640364/donovan-mc-nabb-eagles-retrospective-stupid-people

Sonny Jurgensen or even Davey O'Brien or anyone who didn't puke in the Super Bowl.

Here's the objective record about McNabb. Donovan McNabb holds the Eagles' single-season record for completions, passing yards, and yards per game. He missed out on the single-season touchdown record by one and held the record for passer rating until Nick Foles broke it last year. He holds franchise career records for completions, touchdowns, and yards, and among passers with at least 1,000 attempts, holds the franchise records for completion percentage and passer rating as well. McNabb made six Pro Bowls as an Eagle, twice as many as any other Eagles quarterback in history. McNabb was also the first quarterback in NFL history to throw for 30 or more touchdowns in a season while throwing fewer than 10 interceptions. But we don't talk about that a whole lot.

Judging an individual by team accomplishments, particularly in the NFL, where the best players in the league, even quarterbacks, play less than half of the time, seems remiss. Saying an individual player at any position in any team sport had a more or less impressive career because he won more or fewer games or championships ignores a tremendous amount of context, to say nothing of the fallacy of trying to reduce an entire career down to one drive or one game. It's what people do when they're afraid of information.

But just for fun, let's try it. Let's pretend that Donovan McNabb, and Donovan McNabb alone, was responsible for whether his team won or lost. Let's pretend that it doesn't matter that he was throwing to a quality wide receiver in only two of his five NFC championship game appearances, that McNabb, and not Blaine Bishop, lost Joe Jurevicius over the middle against Tampa Bay, and so on. Let's assume all that.

McNabb lost his only Super Bowl by three points. Sure, he threw three interceptions, but so did Ron Jaworski, Eagles legend, who threw for 66 fewer yards, completed less than half of his passes, and threw two fewer touchdowns in a game that the Eagles lost by 17.

Here are some post-merger Hall of Fame quarterbacks who never came as close as McNabb did to winning a title: Dan Fouts, Warren Moon, Fran Tarkenton, and Dan Marino.

Consider also that McNabb is also the franchise's career leader in wins, with 92. And the Eagles aren't the Dallas Cowboys, which means they don't have a long line of successful quarterbacks. For all the hype about the fans wanting Jeff Garcia over McNabb, Garcia won six games in an Eagles uniform. McNabb won nine *playoff* games with the Eagles.

And I guess you could make an argument that Van Brocklin did win a title, that that's all that matters. And wishing to take nothing away from Van Brocklin, a Hall of Famer in his own right, the NFL in 1960 was very different than it is today. For instance, those Eagles won a title with a 235-pound, thirty-five-year-old Chuck Bednarik playing both center and middle linebacker. And today's defenses are the product of tireless coaches who spend more time developing new wrinkles on the zone blitz than NASA spent putting a man on the moon. Any reasonably good quarterback from a large high school in Texas or Southern California today would make the Pro Bowl in 1960, so great are the advances in strategy, fitness, and training. McNabb was one of the first modern quarterbacks to run out of the shotgun spread, part of the Peyton Manning generation that revolutionized the game around the turn of the century.

Speaking of Peyton Manning, this is my own personal theory, but the real reason McNabb took so much flak was not that he wasn't good. Despite being built like an Easter Island statue, McNabb missed the occasional game with injury, so we had the occasional object lesson in what life would be like without the franchise quarterback, and as beloved as Koy Detmer, A.J. Feeley, and Garcia were for their spot starter duty, most reasonable people understood that McNabb was pretty good.

When McNabb took longer than everyone liked to win a Super Bowl, despite making the playoffs every year, people understandably grew impatient and dissatisfied. That's understandable. In case you haven't figured it out by now, I'm in the 99th percentile of McNabb fanboys, and I'm a little disappointed the Eagles didn't win at least one Super Bowl in the 2000s, when they had McNabb and Dawkins and Westbrook and that great offensive line. Maybe they would have with a better quarterback.

The thing is, if the Eagles had ditched McNabb, they wouldn't have replaced him with Tom Brady or Peyton Manning, and those two, Brett Favre, and Drew Brees are the only quarterbacks who appear ahead of McNabb anywhere on the leaderboards for touchdowns, completions, yards, and, indeed, wins, from the decade of 2000–2009.

In terms of sustained success, Donovan McNabb was at the very worst, the fifth-best quarterback of his generation, behind the all-time leader in passing yards and, going into the 2014 season, touchdowns (Favre), the single-season passing yardage record holder (Brees) and, for my money, the two best football players ever, at any position, from any generation (Manning and Brady). It's tough to be wanted when your competition is that stiff. More on that later.

Donovan McNabb was born November 25, 1976 in Chicago, where he played both football and basketball with some pretty impressive teammates—Simeon Rice in football, Antoine Walker in basketball—at Mount Carmel High School, a Catholic school on the South Side, a few blocks from Lake Michigan.

McNabb went on to play quarterback at Syracuse, which is where his story gets personal for me.

The first NFL player personnel decision I remember having an opinion about was that the Eagles should draft McNabb. I thought they should trade down from No. 2, because they'd be able to get him later in the first round, but I wanted McNabb badly, and here's why.

I grew up a Virginia Tech Hokies fan, and in my formative football years, Tech battled for control of the old Big East primarily with Miami. In the mid-1990s, when I was starting to understand football, Virginia Tech was becoming a nationally significant program for the first time under Frank Beamer, and Miami was in between periods of dominance. That left the Hokies to contend with McNabb's Syracuse teams for the conference title. McNabb played four years at Syracuse, from 1995–98. In 1995, Virginia Tech went 6-1 in the Big East and tied with Miami for the conference title. Syracuse went 5-2. The next year, Syracuse went 6-1 and Virginia Tech went 5-2 and finished second. The year after that, Virginia Tech went 6-1 and Syracuse went 5-2, and in 1998, Syracuse went 6-1 in the conference and the Hokies went 5-2.

And oh my God, McNabb was infuriating. I hated him so much, because Virginia Tech couldn't stop him, no matter what they did, despite defense being the Hokies' calling card. Being a Virginia Tech fan while McNabb was at Syracuse was like having allergies—he'd show up, get in your head, and make you miserable for a couple months, and even though you know he was coming and when, there was nothing you could do to stop him.

By the time McNabb finished his senior season, a season that coincided with Bobby Hoying wearing out his welcome in Eagles green, I wanted badly to have this inexorable quarterback on my team.

And it happened. And boy, were people pissed.

Again, understandably, because as awesome as McNabb was, Ricky Williams was even better in college, and we didn't know then that he'd become the Jimmy Buffett of the NFL, nor did we know then that running backs are largely fungible and expendable if you have a good coach and a good offensive line.

So a radio host with a history of headline-grabbing stunts performed in bad taste, the kind of acts that not only influence thousands of Eagles fans, but also paint thousands more unfairly with their stink, took 30 boors to New York City for the draft, and they booed the selection of McNabb. We might as well have stopped the narrative merry-go-round 15 seconds into McNabb's professional career.

Because their careers overlapped so nicely and because they were so often criticized for the same reasons, McNabb is forever tied to Andy Reid, down to the point where everyone's forgotten about how great the 2000 season was for both of them.

For me, the most impressive McNabb season wasn't 2004, when he threw 31 touchdowns against eight picks and went to the Super Bowl. It was 2000.

Former Eagles linebacker Ike Reese said the injury to Duce Staley forced the defense to take leadership that season, a job that was made easier by McNabb's playmaking ability.

"Having Donovan over there and allowing him to be able to make a play or two or three in the third or fourth quarter to give us the victory," Reese said, "It was great. We knew as a defense that if we kept the game close enough, that Donovan was special enough that he could make something happen, and he did that countless times that season."

McNabb's first year as a starter, he threw 21 touchdowns against 13 interceptions, which doesn't sound like much, but the 2000 Eagles, who scored 351 points and went 11-5, had just an unbelievably bad offense.

The signature moment of that season was its first play. Having gone 5-11 the previous season, the Eagles faced the Cowboys on Opening Day, in Texas Stadium, on a September afternoon whose weather would best be described as "solar." In the sun, the turf was 180 degrees Fahrenheit, a temperature that, until that afternoon, I was sure would melt artificial grass. Andy Reid called for an onside kick to start the game, a call he'd return to throughout his career, and the Eagles recovered.

That afternoon, the Eagles's training staff encouraged the players to drink pickle juice in the hope the saltiness would prevent cramping, and it worked like a charm. Staley ran for more than 200 yards and the Eagles won 41-14.

Staley went down with a broken foot after five games, leaving McNabb with as few skilled position players as you can get on a playoff team. Darnell Autry led the team in rushing attempts. McNabb's top two wide receivers, Charles Johnson and Torrance Small, were castoffs who combined—*combined*, mind you—for 96 catches, 1,211 yards, and 10 touchdowns. If they'd been one person named Charrance Smallson, Smallson would have finished tied for sixth in the NFL in catches and receiving touchdowns, and 13th in receiving yards.

You know how I said earlier that a quarterback isn't the only player on the team? That's not entirely true, because at times McNabb seemed to be the only player on the 2000 Eagles. Only tight end Chad Lewis kept McNabb's 2000 from being an extended game of Kill the Man with the Ball.

Donovan McNabb *(AP Photo/ Joseph Kaczmarek)*

McNabb also led the team in rushing yards and touch-downs—629 of the former, six of the latter—and established himself as the next great scrambling quarterback in the league, en route to his first Pro Bowl and a second-place finish to Marshall Faulk in MVP voting.

McNabb was a good passer—he had tremendous arm strength, took care of the ball, and threw deep well. He wasn't particularly accurate, especially late in his career, when he took a lot of heat for developing what looked like a very good forkball that more often than not bounced in front of receivers. And make no mistake, he deserved all of that criticism.

But what set him apart, particularly early in his career, was his running ability. McNabb at his best was a stronger, faster Brett Favre, able to extend plays with his legs and find the open man after the original routes broke down. (Favre also took heat for inaccuracy and lacking touch on his throws as a young quarterback.)

And that would've been great if McNabb had come along ten years later. As it was, McNabb was the face of the first generation in which a black NFL starting quarterback was commonplace. And in keeping with persistent racial stereotypes, much was made about McNabb's ability to run. It fit with stereotypes about the black scrambling quarterback and the white stand-up pocket passer, with the pernicious, yet unspoken connotations about athleticism versus intelligence.

This is where people who think racism and stereotyping ended in 1968 stuck the "sensitive" label on McNabb, who was keenly aware not only of the lens through which he was viewed, but of his place in history as well. I prefer to say McNabb was image-conscious. He might have continued to run for 600 yards per year if McNabb's running ability was discussed in the same manner as Favre's or Steve Young's. But McNabb had always wanted to be seen as a passer first, and not an athlete, dating back to his college days—he told the *Sporting News* in 2011 that his decision to choose Syracuse over Nebraska had to do with his disinterest in running an option offense.

That opened him up to criticism from the sports media, who would put him in a box if he ran and criticize his sensitivity if he didn't, as well as political commenters from both partisan extremes—Rush Limbaugh and J. Whyatt Mondesire—who were inexplicably given sports media platforms. The booing at the draft had turned into gaslighting, and with relatively high political stakes for football.

From 2001 to 2003, McNabb settled into a routine—play well, win the division, lose in the NFC Championship Game. In 2002, the Eagles ran into the Greatest Show on Turf Rams, and like many teams in those days, played relatively well and lost. The next year, they lost at home to the Tampa Bay Buccaneers, a team they'd owned in previous years, in the last NFL game at Veterans Stadium. That was a shocking and embarrassing loss from which nobody, including McNabb, is free from blame. In 2003–04, they faced the Carolina Panthers and lost, 14-3, without Brian Westbrook.

Conference championship week in 2004 was apparently a bank holiday from pass interference. In the AFC Championship Game, Ty Law, who was a great cover corner, took advantage of this leniency en route to a Patriots win. That night in Philadelphia, Ricky Manning, who wasn't a great cover corner, spent more time with his hands inside Todd Pinkston's jersey than Pinkston did; he drew relatively little attention from the referees, and intercepted three passes. McNabb himself was injured during that game, and overthrew Staley on a wheel route that the younger, faster Westbrook would have tracked down if he were in the game.

McNabb finally got his weapon, Terrell Owens, that off-season, and for a season, they were dynamic. Owens caught 14 touchdown passes before Roy Williams broke Owens's leg with a horse collar tackle in Week 15, while the young Westbrook, liberated from his platoon with Staley and Correll Buckhalter, developed into one of the best running backs in franchise history. The Eagles were 13-1 after that game, after which Reid pulled his starters and lost the last two games, but still recorded a franchise record for wins.

Even without T.O., McNabb and the Eagles still got to the Super Bowl relatively easily. They beat the 8-8 Vikings in the divisional round, and in the NFC Championship Game, they waltzed to a 27-10 defeat of an Atlanta Falcons team that resembled McNabb's first playoff team: comprised of a transcendent dual-threat quarterback, a solid defense, and not much else.

Owens came back for the Super Bowl and caught nine balls for 122 yards on a leg that wasn't anywhere close to healed, and if the Eagles had won, his performance would have been lauded as an all-time Tough Guy performance.

As it was, the rest of the Eagles didn't play lights-out football, which was what it took to beat the Patriots in a big game back then. Westbrook ran fifteen times, but only gained 44 yards, half of them on one play, and in the absence of a credible run game, McNabb threw himself on the rocky shores of a legendary Patriots pass defense, going 30-for-51 for 357 yards and three touchdowns, but also throwing three interceptions in the process. (In his first Super Bowl, Brady threw for 155 yards and won MVP honors . . .)

Lito Sheppard also said McNabb threw up in the fourth quarter, a claim Jon Bois debunked in his post after applying painstaking, Zapruder-like analysis. And as Bois points out, even if McNabb did throw up, 1) So what? and 2) The Eagles scored on that drive anyway.

But that was the peak, and from then on—the disastrous 2005 season with the T.O. meltdown and a series of injuries that limited him to nine games, then disappointments in the next two seasons—it seemed like it was only a matter of time before not only McNabb but Reid as well would wear out his welcome, particularly when the Eagles spent a second-round pick on quarterback Kevin Kolb in 2007.

McNabb's last title push came during a strange 2008–09 season. It didn't start well, and by midseason it looked like the Eagles had turned into a farce. In Week 11, the Eagles tied the Cincinnati Bengals, after which McNabb claimed to have been unaware a game could end like that, a comment for which he's been ridiculed to this day.

The next week, the Eagles lost 36-7 to Baltimore, and Reid replaced an ineffective McNabb with Kolb at halftime. And while Kolb didn't fare any better, the benching led to speculation that Kolb would take over full-time as the starter.

He didn't.

The next week, McNabb threw four touchdowns on a 48-20 Thanksgiving rout of Arizona, and the Eagles, who had started 5-5-1, won four of their last five to sneak into the playoffs. Somewhat surprisingly, the Eagles had the bracket open up for them after that—they went on the road to beat the Vikings and the Giants each by double digits in the first two rounds, and set up a rematch with the Cardinals with a Super Bowl berth on the line.

The first half was an unmitigated disaster—the Eagles fell down 24-6 at the half, but McNabb, despite his reputation as a choker, staged the greatest playoff comeback of his career, leading three touchdown drives in about 16 minutes to put the Eagles on top, 25-24. But this time, it was the stalwart defense that couldn't hold the lead, and the Cardinals went on to win their first conference title.

McNabb played one more season with the Eagles, splitting time not only with Kolb but with Michael Vick as well, and while the Eagles went 11-5, they lost by 20 in a playoff game in Dallas that really wasn't even that close. The next offseason, McNabb was traded to Washington for a pair of draft picks. He played one mediocre season in Washington before being traded to the Vikings to replace Favre the next offseason, where he played another, even less impressive season before retiring at age thirty-five. McNabb has since gone on to work as an analyst for Fox Sports.

McNabb isn't the only instance of a team's best player taking the blame for its failures, and he won't be the last. One day, the Eagles will win a Super Bowl, but until then, we will pick over quarterbacks' flaws on talk radio, on Internet comment sections, and in the corners of Delaware Valley bars. It's the price of doing business for a fan base that neither wanted nor deserved the best offensive player they had ever seen, but got him anyway.

As a forthright, talkative Midwesterner who refused to pander to Philadelphia fans' insatiable desire to be validated, McNabb was perhaps the worst face of a franchise whose fans seem to like players in inverse proportion to their intelligence and volubility.

At least they didn't boo McNabb when he had his number retired. It was literally the least they could do.

Of course, the greatest irony is this: the two biggest strikes against McNabb were that he was overly sensitive and didn't have the ineffable winner's quality.

No Eagles quarterback has ever suffered more criticism, justified and otherwise, than McNabb. And in spite of that, no Eagles quarterback has ever won more.

CHASE UTLEY

11 Calling Chase Utley one of the ten best athletes in Philadelphia history is probably going to shock some people. Yet such a reaction is ridiculous—an examination of Utley's career makes it clear that he's one of the ten best second basemen ever, a surefire Hall of Famer, and the best position player (apart from Mike Schmidt) that the Phillies have ever had.

Relatively few people, including those who have followed him his entire career, seem to be aware of this. Take it from the 2011 edition of the *Baseball Prospectus Annual*:

> "Consider the flukes of circumstance that have made Utley a perennial MVP bridesmaid; the biomechanics that gave him uncharacteristic yips during the playoffs and the myopia of observers who, for perhaps the only time in the history of baseball, have criminally underrated a tough-as-nails dirty-uniform guy . . . "

Chase Utley is adored and revered across baseball, and he is underrated. In Phillies history, only Mike Schmidt has a record of sustained success, relative to position and league, that can rival Utley's. At his peak, Utley was not only the best player on the Phillies, but also the second-best player in the

National League and one of the 10 best second basemen of all time. In a just world, he'd make the Hall of Fame easily, even with his injury history and relatively late start to his career.

Utley was born on December 17, 1978 in Pasadena, California. He was an All-America player at Polytechnic High School, the alma mater of Tony Gwynn and seven-time All-Star shortstop Vern Stephens, as well as Milton Bradley. Utley nearly stayed in Southern California for his entire career, as the Dodgers drafted him in the second round of the 1997 draft. Utley turned down an $850,000 bonus to join another local team, the UCLA Bruins, where he ranks in the top 10 in school history in hits, runs, home runs, and RBI.

After three years at UCLA, Utley tried his luck in the draft once more, this time going No. 15 overall to the Phillies in 2000.

Utley was highly regarded at the time—Dodgers scout Gib Bodet graded Utley's hitting potential as a 70 on the 20-80 scale favored by scouts, and as my Crashburn Alley colleague Eric Longenhagen said, "Scouts do not throw 70s around like Tootsie Rolls at a Halloween parade, they hem and haw and make all sorts of uncomfortable faces before they pen that number on a report. For Bodet to slap a 7 on Utley's bat is, on its own, notable. For him to project it to a 7 all the way from a 4? That's prescient."[4]

It took a while for Utley to get to the majors—as a college player with a relatively early birthday, Utley didn't play his first full season in the pros until he was twenty-two, and his

---

4 For Bodet's full report and Eric's commentary on that and other scouting reports of the young Utley, go here: http://crashburnalley. com/2013/06/04/phillies-draft-retrospective-chase-utley/

arrival in Philadelphia was delayed in two respects by the Scott Rolen trade: first, organizational concern over the departure of Rolen himself led to Utley spending his first season in AAA at third base rather than second, which may or may not have slowed down his development. Second, the only player the Phillies got back from St. Louis who made any sort of impact was Placido Polanco, who was a pretty good second baseman himself.

Utley made the big club for the first time in 2003, then in 2004 and 2005, split time with Polanco while occasionally spelling Jim Thome at first base. In June 2005, the Phillies traded Polanco to the Detroit Tigers, leaving Utley in sole possession of the second base job he'd retain to this day.

In 2005, Utley played 147 games and hit .291/.376/.540, and was the best player (according to WAR, by more than two wins over Jimmy Rollins), on a Phillies team that missed the playoffs by only one game. He finished 13th in MVP voting, third among Phillies behind Rollins and Pat Burrell. Remember that, because it's going to be a pattern.

In 2006, the Phillies again narrowly missed the playoffs, despite Utley putting up another seven-win season, hitting .309/.379/.527. He was two wins better than his teammate Ryan Howard and finished seventh in MVP voting, his highest finish ever. In 2007, Utley hit .332/.410/.566, the best season of his career, despite John Lannan breaking his hand with a pitch in July.

Despite the time off, Utley was, again, almost two wins better than Rollins, who won the MVP, and five wins better than Howard, who finished fifth.

The next year, the Phillies won the World Series and Utley hit .292/.380/.535, and despite finishing in a virtual dead heat with Albert Pujols for the league lead in WAR, finished tied for 14th in MVP voting, one spot ahead of Ryan Ludwick, while Howard (1.8 WAR) finished second and Brad Lidge (2.5 WAR) finished eighth.

In 2009, Utley hit .292/.397/.508 for 8.2 WAR, while Howard hit .279/.360/.571 for 3.8 WAR. Howard was third in MVP voting, Utley eighth.

Utley was preposterously good in those five years, and while he made the All-Star team every year, never finished higher than seventh in MVP voting. Put another way, here are the top five WAR totals among National League players from 2005–2009:

1. Albert Pujols: 44.5
2. Chase Utley: 39.5
3. David Wright: 27.2
4. Carlos Beltran: 27.0
5. Chipper Jones: 24.8

Utley trails Pujols by a non-trivial five wins, then laps the rest of the field. And as the BP comment insinuated, it's entirely bizarre for a player like Utley, someone who played for good teams in a big media market, got his jersey dirty, played hard, and posted spectacular seasons to be underrated, but here we are. Why was he so underrated?

Implicit in the question of how Utley came to be underrated is the question of what made him so great. The short answer is that he had no weaknesses. Well, he had two: health, as nagging injuries kept him off the field full-time after age 30; and his throwing arm, which was pretty awful, but as a second baseman, was the weakest part of his game, and one for which he compensated by becoming a dead shot with the glove flip.

Chase Utley *(AP Photo/Chris Szagola)*

In the mid-2000s, Utley looked like he was developing Chuck Knoblauch's disease, where a second baseman suddenly becomes unable to make the throw to first. One Utley throwing error cost the Phillies Game 1 of the 2009 NLCS, in fact. On shorter throws, Utley developed the habit of flipping the ball to first base underhand with his glove, like a soft lacrosse pass. This is a standard technique for infielders when the throw is too short to make at full speed, such as on double play transfers or a first baseman tossing to a pitcher covering on a bunt.

Utley, rather than an easy lob, would make the glove flip to Howard on a line from as far away as 50 or 60 feet.

But apart from those minor weaknesses, Utley's game had almost no holes.

His greatest attribute, particularly as a young player, was his bat speed. Utley, listed at six-foot-one 200 pounds, isn't a particularly large man by modern standards, even for a second baseman, though he towers over Rollins, his double play partner. Utley's swing is also extremely short and quick—he holds his hands low, in a slight crouch, bat vertical, then whips it through the zone, bringing the bat to horizontal, then vertical on the follow-through, with the quickness of a lightswitch. Howard's swing, while productive in its prime, has a long, elegant, almost golflike swoop to it. Utley's swing is direct, violent, and characterized by almost instantaneous hip rotation, like a hockey shot.

That bat speed allows Utley to generate fantastic pull power out of a short swing and a medium-sized body—double-digit home runs in his first 10 full seasons, 30 or more home runs three times, and 40 or more doubles three times. Utley's career slugging percentage is higher than Reggie Jackson's.

Once Utley gets on base, he's one of the best baserunners of all time. Going into the 2014 season, he was the best percentage basestealer in history with at least 100 attempts, including going 23-for-23 in 2009 and 14-for-14 in 2011. Mike Trout passed him in the spring of 2014 and will probably retain the lead for the foreseeable future.

In the field and on the bases, Utley is very much like fellow famous UCLA second baseman Jackie Robinson in terms of taking calculated risks and unorthodox and aggressive plays to steal a base here on offense or an out there on defense.

Let me describe Utley in probably his two most famous highlights. The first came on August 9, 2006. With his team down 3-2 to Atlanta in the top of the seventh, Utley came up against lefty Macay McBride and, using that fast-twitch hip action, blasted a bases-clearing opposite-field double to put the Phillies up 5-3. On the next pitch, Ryan Howard tagged a Baltimore chop out in front of the plate, and McBride drifted over near first base to catch it and throw Howard out. Meanwhile, Utley had run full-speed around third base and snuck in just under the tag to score from second base on a groundout for the fifth of what would be eight runs in the inning.

Utley's baserunning on that play prompted Phillies announcer Harry Kalas to coin one of the last iconic catchphrases of his career: "Chase Utley, you are the man!"

The second highlight came in Game 5 of the 2008 World Series, after a 46-hour rain delay necessitated an unprecedented three-inning sprint to the finish with the World Series title on the line. With two out in the seventh inning, the game tied 3-3 and the go-ahead run, Jason Bartlett, on second base, Tampa Bay's Akinori Iwamura bounced a ball up the middle. Utley cut it off, and with his momentum carrying him toward center field, would have to hustle to get Iwamura at first.

Perhaps realizing this, or sensing the possibility for a misplay, Rays third base coach Tom Foley sent Bartlett home in a move almost identical to the "Chase Utley, you are the man!" play. The difference is that while McBride made sure of the out at first, Utley noticed Bartlett rounding third, pump-faked to first, and then threw home. By this point, Utley was on the shortstop side of the bag and moving the wrong way, and his throw bounced in front of Carlos Ruiz, who collected it and tagged Barlett out to end the inning. Eric Bruntlett scored in the bottom of the 7th, and the Phillies won Philadelphia's first major league championship in any sport since 1983.

Utley is by all accounts a well-liked teammate and a respected member of the community—as most athletes of Utley's fame undertake charitable projects, Utley and his wife set up a foundation to prevent animal cruelty. Utley also achieved a degree of notoriety when a character in It's Always Sunny in Philadelphia wrote an embarrassing fan letter to him, and Utley became to that show what Keith Hernandez was to Seinfeld when he made a cameo appearance in 2010, then wrote a response in 2013. The closest Utley's come to generating negative headlines was his habit of saying the f-word into a hot mic on live television, once at the Home Run Derby in 2008, then later that year at the Phillies' World Series parade, a pair of faux pas that probably only made diehard fans love him more.

Utley has the All-Star appearances, the postseason heroics (the 2008 play, a World Series ring, a career .902 postseason OPS, and in 2009 he hit a record-tying five home runs in the World Series), and all the trappings of a superstar.

Which returns us to the original question: how did Utley become so underrated?

First of all, Utley is kind of an awkward-looking player. He doesn't look physically impressive, doesn't run with the power of Mike Trout or field with the elegance of Andrelton Simmons or swing with the grace of Ken Griffey. He runs kind of funny, with his elbows out, and shuffles from side to side like a crab in the field, and for as effective as his swing is, it looks unorthodox. There's a little bit of Hunter Pence's awkwardness to Utley's game.

And for as intense a player as Utley is, he's not particularly charismatic or demonstrative on the field—even after doubling and scoring from second on a grounder to the pitcher in the iconic highlight from 2006, Utley, then only twenty-seven, slid into home, popped up, then walked calmly to the dugout. No pantomimed safe sign, no shouting, no leap of joy.

Utley's walk-up music, at least as long as I can remember, has been the opening riff to Led Zeppelin's "Kashmir," which is the kind of song you play when you're wearing sunglasses and a leather jacket and carrying a shotgun, walking away from a burning building and not looking back when it explodes. It communicates not only menace, but coolness, and it fits Utley perfectly. Even though Utley carried a leadership role on the Phillies during their dynasty, it was usually Jimmy Rollins, or sometimes Cole Hamels or Ryan Howard who delivered the key quote.

In addition to not being particularly colorful, most people probably legitimately didn't know how good Utley was in his prime, which seems like a weird thing to say about a five-time All-Star. If Utley had come along 10 years later, that wouldn't have been the case.

First of all, Utley's entire career took place post-*Moneyball* and in the heyday of Bill James, Baseball Prospectus, and the rest of the statistical revolution in baseball, but in 2014, the war against innumeracy and illogic in sports media and fandom has largely been won—if you don't know what I mean by this, skip ahead to the chapter on Wilt Chamberlain—and we're just mopping up the last pockets of resistance.

In 2007, however, that war was still very much in progress. A lot of analysis and color commentary rested on pitcher wins and RBI, or even broad strokes and hoary clichés that would sound like pidgin Nietzchean philosophy if the people spouting those clichés didn't think Nietzche played linebacker for the Green Bay Packers in the 1960s.

Jimmy Rollins won the MVP in 2007 because round numbers mattered then, as did "leadership," which Rollins provided in the form of an inspirational quote at the season's start. Ryan Howard finished in the top five in MVP voting four times because baseball writers attributed the 572 runs he drove in from 2006–2010 to Howard's skill as a "run producer" rather than affected by the fact that Utley was often on base in front of him.

Then there's defense. Around the time Utley came up, the baseball community started taking defensive analysis seriously, and the results have been illuminating. FanGraphs judges defense on UZR, which is based on coding defensive plays by type and position based on video evidence.

UZR data exists back to 2002, and Utley is the best defensive second baseman it's ever evaluated, both in total runs saved and runs saved per 150 games.

Baseball Reference, whose flavor of WAR I've used throughout the book, uses Total Zone to evaluate defense. Total Zone takes box score data to see how many outs a player records and compares him to his contemporaries, which allows defenders to be rated back to the 1910s. By that method, Utley has produced 17.1 wins' worth of value with his glove alone, the sixth-highest total ever for a second baseman, even though Utley played 600 fewer games than anyone above him on the list. Utley's defense has been worth 17.1 WAR, while Ryan Howard, taken as a whole, has a career total WAR of 19.0.

Contrast that to Utley's reputation at the time as a defensive butcher. And we didn't know any better—his throwing problems were long evident, he looked awkward in the field, and he played relatively deep and positioned himself well so he never needed to make the kind of spectacular, diving stop you need to make more often when your positioning or first step is lacking.

Utley also suffered because, since we didn't know about his defense at the time, he didn't have that one eye-popping skill to hang his hat on, like Howard with his power. From 2006–2009 or so, Ryan Howard was probably the best pure power hitter in baseball, and everyone knew that about him.

From 2005–2010, Utley was a good hitter who hit for good power and stole some, though not an eye-popping number, of bases and posted a good, though not astounding, OBP.

Even Utley's on-base skills went under the radar because, 2007 excepted, he never hit for a huge average and walked a lot, but never 100 times a year—he got on base as often as he did in large part because he got hit by a lot of pitches (157 for his career as I write, tied for 12th-most all-time). The one all-time record he ever held was for stolen base percentage, which I personally think is really cool, but it isn't as sexy as home runs. Utley never won a batting title or a home run title—he led the league in runs scored in 2006, then in HBP in each of the next three years, and has never led the league in any other category.

Utley wasn't a full-time regular until he was twenty-six, and after he turned thirty, he started missing huge chunks of time for knee and hip injuries, which shortened his career on both ends and depressed his career counting stats.

There's not an easy quality you can point to illustrate Utley's greatness—you need to see the whole picture, and seeing the whole picture can be difficult.

When you do, however, this is what you get: one of the 10 best second basemen ever, one of the best players of his generation at any position, the best player of the best period in Phillies history, and the best position player the Phillies have ever produced, apart from Mike Schmidt.

And a no-doubt Hall of Famer.

It's quite a picture.

JULIUS ERVING

12 Aside from his propensity for dunking and hitting the baseline layup, one of the things that best defines Julius Erving is his nickname, "Dr. J." Up until the 1950s, when it was determined that not everyone needed a nickname (and not all nicknames needed to be alliterative), baseball players had the best nicknames. Since then, basketball players' nicknames have come to be of immense importance in terms of shaping a narrative about the player. Not all players get a great one, but even those who don't wind up on a first-name basis with fans and media, like beloved uncles or Brazilian soccer players: LeBron, Dirk, Wilt, Kareem, Kobe. Sometimes the nickname sticks, but doesn't replace the given name—The Answer, His Airness, Sir Charles—but sometimes it does.

This happened to Magic Johnson, who was blessed with a wonderful nickname, one that described his skill and charisma and fit to the point where it all but replaced his given name. It also happened to Julius Erving. The story you probably know by now: the nickname didn't come from his intelligence, or the clinical nature in which he scored, because if we were giving Erving a nickname based on style of play, it would probably be closer to something metaphysical than scientific. No, the young Julius Erving had a boyhood friend whom he called "The Professor," and the friend called him "The Doctor" in return. As a pickup hoops star, Erving saw the nickname extended to "Doctor Julius" and then truncated to "Dr. J."

And now, twenty years after his retirement, referring to him as "Erving" on second reference, as per usual practice, is awkward enough that I'm just going to call him Dr. J throughout. His nickname is so well-known, so mellifluous, so cool, in short, that typing his actual legal name requires me to break my train of thought and make an effort. If I had a nickname as cool as "Dr. J," I'd forget my real name.

But moving on to his style of play, in particular the aforementioned baseline layup.

If you know one thing about the 1980 NBA Finals, you know that in Game 6, with Kareem out with a broken ankle, Magic Johnson, a twenty-year-old rookie guard, started at center and dropped 42 points, 15 rebounds, and seven assists on the Sixers to eliminate them from the playoffs on their own home floor.

The second thing you should know about the 1980 Finals is that in the fourth quarter of Game 4, Dr. J scored one of the most incredible, athletic baskets you'll ever see. He drove Lakers center Mark Landsberger to the baseline, on the far right side of the backboard. From there, Dr. J gathered his dribble and palmed the ball in his right hand, took two steps past Landsberger, and leapt into the air parallel to the baseline and twisted 180 degrees to face the court. Ball still in his outstretched right arm, he attempted to put it in off the glass on the near side, but found himself behind the backboard, so Erving pulled the ball back, ducked under the basket, and flung the ball off the window, past Kareem and in. Then, after having been in the air longer than the crew of Apollo 11, Dr. J landed softly on the floor before tripping either over his own feet or those of Laker Jim Chones and falling to the floor.

Dr. J was born on Long Island on February 22, 1950. After high school, he took a scholarship from the University of Massachusetts, where he spent one year on the freshman team, as NCAA rules dictated at the time, then entered the varsity starting lineup as a sophomore in 1969–70. And he wrecked house: in two seasons at UMass, Dr. J averaged 38.4 minutes a game (regulation college games are only 40 minutes, remember, not 48 as they are in the NBA) and made the most of them, going for 26.2 points and 20.2 rebounds as a six-foot-six wing player.

During the early 1970s, the NBA underwent a challenge for supremacy in professional basketball from the American Basketball Association, an outlaw league if ever there were one. While the NBA embraced a certain conservative aesthetic (one could say stodgy or "Boston Celtics-like" in a less charitable moment), the ABA was Xanadu: a red-white-and-blue basketball, innovations like the dunk contest and three-point line that the NBA wouldn't embrace for years, and no defense.

Dr. J, who left college one year before he became eligible for the NBA draft, signed with the Virginia Squires of the ABA, and almost immediately became the best player in the league: his leaping ability and charisma made him an instant fan favorite, and in five seasons in the ABA, Dr. J was named second-team All-ABA once and first-team All-ABA four times. He won three scoring titles, three MVP awards, and a championship in 1974 with the New York Nets.

It was hardly a foregone conclusion that Dr. J would join the Sixers when he jumped to the NBA: the Milwaukee Bucks drafted him in 1972, but when he attempted to switch leagues that season, he signed with the Atlanta Hawks. Unsatisfied with his Squires contract, Dr. J worked out a deal with Atlanta, but his ABA team successfully sued to prevent him from joining any other team. He missed 13 games in 1972–73, but Dr. J eventually returned to Virginia for the rest of the season and won his first MVP award. After the season, unable to keep the league's brightest star in the relatively small market of Norfolk, Virginia, the Squires traded him to the Nets, where he remained for the next three years.

When the NBA and ABA merged before the 1976–77 season, four teams made the move, including Dr. J's Nets, while the rest folded. But again, Dr. J found himself in the middle of a contract dispute, and the Nets, having just forked over a $3.2 million expansion fee to the NBA, plus another $4.8 million to the Knicks for violating their territorial rights, plus being faced with receiving no television revenue for three years, couldn't afford to keep their star. They offered to sell Dr. J to the Knicks for $4.8 million to offset the territorial fee, but the Knicks said no, leaving the Nets to sell their franchise player to the Sixers for $3 million.

So when Dr. J joined the Sixers in the NBA in 1976, the league had 22 teams, four of which had had either a claim to Dr. J or a clear-cut opportunity to acquire him before he ended up in Philadelphia.

It worked out okay from there. When he arrived in Philadelphia, the Sixers were planning on retiring No. 32, the number Dr. J had worn in college and in the ABA, in honor of Billy Cunningham, who had retired the previous season, so Dr. J took No. 6, which he would wear for the rest of his career.

In 1975–76, the Sixers were okay, finishing 46-36 and losing in the first round of the playoffs. They featured former No. 1 overall pick Doug Collins and jump-shooter Lloyd (later "World B.") Free in the backcourt, Joe "Jelly Bean" Bryant (father of Kobe) at forward, and a center tandem of Darryl Dawkins and shot blocker Caldwell Jones—a rotation of "Jelly Bean," "Chocolate Thunder," "Dr. J," and "World B. Free" might make the 1976–77 Sixers the best team in NBA history for nicknames—and then they started adding pieces.

In addition to Dr. J, the Sixers poached another forward, George McGinnis, from the ABA, giving them the last four MVPs and last four scoring champions in ABA history. They also bought point guard Henry (father of Mike) Bibby from

New Orleans and drafted Mike (father of Mike Jr.) Dunleavy out of the University of South Carolina to back him up.

Coach Gene Shue ran a deep rotation with his young team—the top 11 Sixers in minutes played were all under thirty, and only Steve Mix was older than twenty-seven—and the Sixers responded: six different players averaged double-digit points per game, led by Dr. J with 21.6 and McGinnis with 21.4, and the Sixers finished sixth in the NBA in offensive efficiency and fourth in defensive efficiency en route to winning 50 games, the Atlantic Division, and the Eastern Conference. In his first NBA Finals, Dr. J led the series in scoring, minutes, and steals, while also pacing the Sixers in assists as they fell to the Portland Trail Blazers in six games.

Dr. J was an absolutely stellar, legendary player in the NBA, but he never reached the same individual heights he reached with the Nets. This is due to several factors: first, the quality of play wasn't as good in the early 1970s in the ABA as it was in the late 1970s and early 1980s in the NBA. Second, Dr. J's offensive game, while effective and spectacular, was somewhat limited. Dr. J scored based on his own athleticism and tremendous body control. In the air, he had the body control we usually associate with a very good soccer striker or a figure skater, except he was also six-foot-six and in terms of ability to just fling himself into the air, he could match anyone. He and David Thompson were the natural predecessors to Michael Jordan, in case you were wondering where he came from.

Julius Erving

The problem with that is twofold: an offensive game based entirely on quickness, body control, and leaping ability breaks down as the body breaks down in the late 20s and early 30s. Additionally, Dr. J never developed a reliable jump shot, and while he was a competent passer, he was never Magic Johnson. Without a finesse game to fall back on, he aged less gracefully than he might have—in the modern game, we could look at Kobe Bryant's aging pattern against that of Dwyane Wade or Allen Iverson for a case study.

But Dr. J brought the flair and style of the ABA to a league that needed it badly. Bill Simmons, in his *The Book of Basketball*, called Dr. J one of the nine most important NBA players ever:

"It's like Apple with home computers, Bill James with baseball statistics, Lorne Michaels with sketch comedy . . . maybe the seeds for the revolution were in place, but somebody had to have the foresight to water those seeds and see what would happen. For basketball, that person ended up being Doc."

That high-scoring quartet of Dr. J, Collins, McGinnis, and Free took the Sixers back to first place and the playoffs in 1978, where they lost to the Bullets in the Eastern Conference finals. Six games into the season, the Sixers replaced Shue as head coach with Cunningham, who turned the Sixers into the league's top offense. After that season, they started to turn the roster over, trading McGinnis for Bobby Jones and Ralph Simpson (Note: I did a double-take too, but this isn't Ralph Sampson, legendary Virginia Cavaliers and Houston Rockets center) and drafting Maurice Cheeks. They also offloaded Free to San Diego for a first-round draft pick in 1984, a trade that must have seemed bizarre at the time, but eventually netted the Sixers Charles Barkley. They lost in the Eastern Conference semifinals.

In 1979–80, Dr. J left to carry the scoring load on his own and dropped 26.9 points per game, the highest total of his NBA career, on 51.9 percent from the floor, then a career high in any league. The Sixers won 59 games and breezed to the NBA finals, where Dr. J dropped his baseline reverse in Game 4, then lost to Magic Johnson, center, in six games.

Playoff defeat was becoming a particular signature of Dr. J's by this point. The next season, Dr. J, in his age-thirty season, led the Sixers in points and blocks and was second on the team in rebounds, steals, and assists to win his only NBA MVP award.

The Sixers won 62 games and still finished behind the Celtics in the Atlantic Division, then lost to Boston in a legendarily close seven-game Eastern Conference finals series: five of the seven games were decided by two points or less, including a one-point Game 7 loss at the Garden. In 2013, John Hollinger of ESPN called this series the best of the post-merger era.

In 1980–81, the Sixers also picked up one of the missing pieces: rookie shooting guard Andrew Toney, the complementary scorer Dr. J had missed since the McGinnis trade in 1978. Toney put a down payment on the nickname "The Boston Strangler" as a rookie in 1981, but in 1982, he finally put the Celtics to bed. The 1981–82 season saw Dr. J and the Sixers more or less repeat their performance from the year before, but in 1982, it was the Sixers, led by Toney's 22.1 points per game, who took the series in seven games from Boston before losing in the Finals, again, to the Lakers, again, in six games, again.

One of the major obstacles Dr. J's Sixers faced was that whenever they reached the NBA Finals, they ran their own solid NBA bigs (Dawkins and Caldwell Jones) against a Hall of Fame center (Walton in 1977, Kareem in 1980 and 1982). As good as Dr. J and his running mates—Collins, McGinnis, Free, Bobby Jones, Cheeks and Toney—were in the backcourt, the Sixers got eaten alive inside, consistently, which not only put them at a disadvantage at center, but made things tough on Toney and Dr. J, who scored close to the basket rather than spacing the floor and shooting threes.

So in the summer of 1982, Sixers GM Pat Williams, after watching his big men get tossed around by monsters, went out and got a monster of his own, 6-foot-10 Moses Malone, the reigning NBA MVP and rebounding champion. Williams sent Caldwell Jones and a first-round pick to Houston as compensation, and emboldened by Malone, the Sixers went on an absolute rampage.

In 1982–83, the Sixers went 65-17, beating the Celtics for the division title by nine games. They outscored their opponents by an average of almost eight points a game. Malone won another rebounding title and another MVP award while forming a prolific scoring trio with Dr. J and Toney: Malone went for 24.5 points per game, with Dr. J scoring 21.4 ppg and Toney chipping in 19.7.

Dr. J, Malone, and Cheeks all started the All-Star Game, while Toney came off the bench behind some "scrub" named Isiah Thomas. Dr. J led all scorers with 25 points and came home with MVP honors in a 132-123 win for the East.

As comprehensively as the Sixers dominated the NBA in the regular season, things only got better in the playoffs. Before the playoffs, the ordinarily taciturn Malone uttered the most famous non-practice-related quote in franchise history: "Fo', Fo', Fo'." While Malone meant only that the Sixers would win the four three-game series required to take home the title, the quote was interpreted as Malone predicting that the Sixers would not only win, but also sweep all three series.

And if the Sixers hadn't blown a fourth-quarter lead in Game 4 of the Eastern Conference Finals against Milwaukee, they'd have done precisely that.

In their third crack at the Lakers in four years, the Sixers finally got over the hump, sweeping Los Angeles in four straight not-particularly-close games. Malone pulled down 72 rebounds, more than any two Lakers combined, and led all scorers in three of the four games in the series. Cheeks, Dr. J, and Toney all averaged at least 15 points and five assists a game, and a 115-108 win at the Forum on May 31 gave the Sixers their first title since 1967, and the last title by any major Philadelphia pro team until 2008.

It was the crowning moment of Dr. J's career.

From that point on, Dr. J declined gracefully, averaging 19.5 points per game over his final four seasons. His team wasn't so fortunate. For the first eight years after Dr. J arrived, the Sixers made up the class of the NBA, along with the Lakers and Celtics, but since then, they've only really mounted two credible title challenges.

Dr. J's Sixers failed to defend their 1983 title, going out in the first round to Dr. J's old team, the Nets. That summer, they drafted Charles Barkley, and returned to the conference finals, but lost to Boston in five games. By that point, the core that had won a title two years before was already coming apart. Toney suffered a foot injury that essentially ended his career at age 27, Jones declined rapidly and retired after the 1986 season. That summer, the Sixers traded Malone to the Washington Bullets, calling time on one of the proudest eras in franchise history. At this point, Dr. J announced the 1986–87 season would be his last.

The next year, Dr. J, thirty-six, played a career-low 60 games and scored a career-low 16.8 points per game. In his last game, a 102-89 Sixers playoff loss to the Milwaukee Bucks, he dropped 24 points to lead all scorers.

We talk about legacy with athletes when we try to talk around what they actually achieved, but Dr. J's legacy might be his greatest achievement. He was the face of the ABA, the most fun, most exciting player of his era, the catalyst for the high-flying, trash-talking, airwalking generation of wings that followed, including, most notably, Michael Jordan.

In the ABA's final season, Dr. J competed in the world's first professional slam dunk contest, which he won over David Thompson with a dunk from the foul line, a move that Jordan used more than a decade later to win the NBA's Slam Dunk Contest. That 1976 competition pitted Dr. J against David Thompson in the final, which must have been like watching two building-sized robots fight each other in midtown Manhattan.

Almost a decade later, after Dr. J, Thompson, and a host of other high-flying ABA stars had made the transition to the NBA, the NBA instituted its own Slam Dunk Contest. In 1984, Dr. J, a month from his thirty-fourth birthday, hung in until the final before capitulating to winner Larry Nance.

There are stats that define players: Wilt Chamberlain's 100 points in a game, Jordan's six titles, Oscar Robertson's triple double for a season.

Here's what I'd pick for Dr. J: he made the All-Star team literally every year of his professional career. All-Star games are mostly about quality and consistency, but popularity and cool factor matter more at the margins. Dr. J was a great and consistent player, and nobody was cooler.

CHARLES BARKLEY

13 You could probably describe Charles Barkley as proto-Iversonian. Both carried mediocre Sixers teams that would've been unwatchable otherwise. Both were undersized for their positions and yet capable of stupendous feats of athleticism. Both cultivated a conspicuously strong sense of self-image, which gave both Iverson and Barkley the capacity to speak out on any subject, candidly, and without fear of the consequence. That tendency got both men in trouble, both in the trivial, public relations sense of the word and in more serious terms as well.

But even leaving out the fact that Barkley might be the most quotable NBA player of his generation, there's plenty to wonder at on the court alone.

Charles Barkley seems to belong to basketball culture as a whole more than he does any pro city, but while he's outgrown his Alabama roots to a certain extent, he hasn't forgotten them, like Larry Bird's more interesting, more Southern brother. Barkley was born on February 20, 1963 in Leeds, Alabama, a smallish suburb of Birmingham. Like Michael Jordan, Barkley was a late bloomer—he only attracted the attention of major college scouts as a high school senior—but while both went to nearby state schools, Jordan's North Carolina Tar Heels had something of a more established basketball tradition than Barkley's Auburn Tigers.

Barkley, suffice it to say, was not your typical collegiate power forward. He cultivated a reputation as a ferocious in-game dunker and tenacious rebounder, and while his numbers were impressive—14.1 points per game, 9.6 assists per game for his collegiate career—what made Barkley stand out was less what he did than the way he did it.

You see, "The Round Mound of Rebound" is a terrible nickname—"Turrible," as Sir Charles himself might say. As a general rule, if your nickname is long enough to rhyme with itself three times, it's too long. Nevertheless, it's descriptive. Barkley played like a fairly typical skilled power forward—perhaps not a good enough shooter to count as a modern stretch four, but we've certainly seen the likes of him before. What made him different was his size. Barkley would've been undersized for a power forward at his listed height of six-foot-six anyway, and it's generally accepted that Barkley, like Iverson, exaggerated his own height by at least an inch or two. Then there's his weight. Barkley came to Auburn after having recently undergone a growth spurt and just kept eating even after he stopped growing, at one point ballooning to almost 300 pounds. (In fact, it's said that Bobby Knight left Barkley off the 1984 Olympic team because of concerns about his weight.) Basketball players tend to be long and lean, like Julius Erving, Barkley's future

Sixers teammate and a player whose offensive game was actually somewhat similar to Barkley's.

But Barkley himself was nearly spherical. By the time he was in his later Auburn years, Barkley wasn't fat anymore, but he always looked somewhat doughy. His short neck, signature shaved head, and tendency to sweat liberally made him look like Marlon Brando in *Apocalypse Now*.

Not that any of that hurt Barkley at all. Barkley's career at Auburn overlapped with Bo Jackson's, briefly making that Alabama land grant college the world's leader in "How does someone that big move that fast?"

Barkley left Auburn after three seasons and inserted himself into a pretty remarkable draft class, a draft class that contained probably four of the top 30 players ever to play the game: Barkley, Jordan, Hakeem Olajuwon, and John Stockton. The Sixers had three first-round picks that year, including the fifth overall pick, obtained six years earlier for shooting guard World B. Free, who was in his own right something of a legend among high-scoring, bald, quotable Sixers. With Jordan and the top three collegiate centers—Olajuwon, Kentucky's Sam Bowie, and North Carolina's Sam Perkins—off the board, the Sixers grabbed Barkley, and he paid off immediately.

Barkley joined a Sixers team that was a mere 18 months removed from going 65-17 and winning the NBA title on the back of a 12-1 playoff run (the "Fo', Fi', Fo" team). But that team wasn't set up for lasting success. Its legendary starting forwards, Erving and Bobby Jones, were winding down their careers. Shooting guard Andrew Toney, who should've been the transitional star between Dr. J and Barkley, began to suffer the same kind of persistent foot injuries that cut Bill Walton's career short.

Barkley's rookie year, the Sixers still went 58-24, and Barkley slid easily into the supporting scoring and rebounding role Jones had filled in the Sixers' best years of the previous decade.

Barkley recorded the first of more than 700 career double-doubles in his third game, scoring 20 points and grabbing 10 rebounds in only 24 minutes against New Jersey. In his 12th game he pulled down a season-high 19 boards against Larry Nance and the Suns. Barkley finished his first season as a first-team All-Rookie selection, along with Bowie, Jordan, Olajuwon, and Perkins, the first five selections in the draft. He played in all 82 games, starting 60, and finished fourth on the team in minutes and points, third in steals, second in rebounds (despite Moses Malone not leaving that many rebounds for other people) and, despite his height, third in blocked shots.

As a twenty-one-year-old rookie, Barkley was an unqualified success, and he only got better, and rapidly: Barkley wouldn't average fewer than 20 points per game until 1996–97, and he would never again average fewer than 10 rebounds a game.

The next season placed the Sixers in transition. Head coach Billy Cunningham, who had been, like Barkley, an undersized power forward who could jump out of the gym and pull down 20 and 10 without any undue exertion, left the team and was replaced by Matt Guokas. Barkley was one of four future Hall of Famers in the Sixers' frontcourt that season, but Erving and Bob McAdoo weren't scoring 30 points per game anymore. Barkley and Malone, however, made a remarkable pair of bigs: Malone pulled down 23.8 points and 11.8 rebounds per game, while Barkley chipped in with 20 points and 12.8 boards per game on 57.2 percent shooting. Between the two of them, Barkley and Malone collected an average of nine offensive rebounds per game. On April 4, the twenty-three-year-old Barkley recorded another milestone, his first of 24 triple-doubles, a mark that places him ninth since the 1985–86 season.

That offseason, however, Malone was traded to Washington, and the Sixers went from a 54-win team in 1985–86 to a 47-win team in 1986–87. Barkley found himself picking up some of the slack, collecting a career-high 14.6 rebounds per game, which led the league, but Barkley himself missed 14 games and the Sixers' season-long rebounding edge was cut by two-thirds. Despite the time off, Barkley was first or second on the team in almost every counting category: points, rebounds, steals, assists, blocks, field goals, and minutes, and Barkley again led the Sixers in scoring and rebounding in the playoffs, as they lost a deciding fifth game to Milwaukee in the first round.

Barkley made his first of 11 consecutive All-Star teams and was named second-team All-NBA at season's end, and followed up his seven 20-rebound games in 1985–86 with 12 in 1986–87. He also recorded five more triple-doubles.

Charles Barkley *(AP Photo/Rusty Kennedy)*

That offseason, Dr. J retired, sending the Sixers into even more of a rebuilding phase. Barkley led the league in offensive rebounds, scored a career-high 28.3 points per game, and wore himself out for a team that went 36-46. Barkley finished the season behind only Michael Jordan in minutes played, and they were tough minutes: Barkley went to the foul line 951 times, by far the most in the league—only 15 other players went to the line even half as often as Barkley did. He also led the league in true shooting percentage and finished 14th in usage rate—Barkley finished sixth in MVP voting, but he was one of the most important players to his team that year.

Barkley had by this point matured into one of the NBA's most consistent performers: in his final seven seasons with the Sixers, Barkley averaged 24.7 points, 12.1 rebounds, and 4 assists and 1.7 steals per game, and apart from one big year each in scoring and rebounding, he never deviated much from those totals. Barkley always played huge minutes and shot for a shockingly high percentage. Among players with at least 1,000 field goal attempts, Barkley is second in Sixers history in PER and field goal percentage, trailing only Wilt Chamberlain in both cases, and in true shooting percentage, Barkley has the top mark in franchise history by 36 points.

After hitting rock bottom in 1987–88, the Sixers fired Guokas and hired Jim Lynam, who brought the Sixers back to the play-offs the next three years, winning a division title in 1989–90, and making the Eastern Conference semifinals that year and the next, where, in both cases, they lost to Jordan's Bulls.

As the Sixers were beginning to come back to the pack, Barkley was involved in his greatest on-court controversy. On March 26, 1991, Barkley spat into the crowd as a response to racist verbal abuse, missing his intended target and hitting an eight-year-old girl in the stands. After incurring a one-game suspension and a $10,000 fine, Barkley sat down with Pat Riley for an interview later that week, in which he apologized for his actions, and didn't stop there.

"'Well, they pay the money, they can do whatever they want to.' No, that's not right," Barkley said. "That's not fair to me as a person. I don't think that because a guy pays $35 for a ticket, he can call me every name in the book. That's not right, and they can't tell me that's right. Just like they complain that I curse and use abusive language, they should throw the fans out of the game. Certain fans come for one simple reason: just to harass you."

When Riley responded: "You don't think you're a role model, do you?" Barkley came back with a variation on the refrain that would become to him what "Float like a butterfly, sting like a bee" was to Muhammad Ali.

"I don't think professional athletes should be role models," Barkley said. "I think parents should be role models. I think that I have an ability to run and dunk a basketball. But there are a million guys who can run and dunk a basketball who are in jail . . . And if I'm a role model, that's fine. But I hope that if I do something wrong, I hope the parents are intelligent enough to tell their kids, 'Charles is wrong.'"

Barkley's last season in Philadelphia turned out to be an eventful one. For starters, Barkley spent time playing next to Manute Bol, which must be the greatest height difference between center and power forward in NBA history. Barkley averaged 23.1 points and 11.1 rebounds per game in 1991–92 and was named not only to the All-Star and All-NBA teams, but to the Dream Team as well, where he famously expressed concern for Angola's basketball team before elbowing forward Herlander Coimbra during one of the most lopsided games in Olympic history. (Coimbra became a celebrity in his home country thanks to the incident and actually became friends with Barkley in later years.)

Barkley led the Dream Team in scoring and scored 30 points, at the time an Olympic record, in a group stage game against Brazil. Among Barkley's teammates on the Dream Team was Magic Johnson, who announced that he had HIV in late 1991. The climate of Johnson's announcement was such that not only did most Americans not accept or tolerate homosexuality, but also many still believed HIV could only be contracted through drug use or gay sex. Barkley, among NBA players, was one of the most supportive of Johnson, speaking publicly on his behalf and asking the Sixers to temporarily unretire Cunningham's No. 32 so he could wear it to honor Johnson.

The 1991–92 season was the most eventful of Barkley's career to that point, even before a 35-47 finish led to the Sixers cleaning house. They fired Lynam and, a month before the Olympics, at Barkley's request, traded their star forward to the Phoenix Suns for Jeff Hornacek, Andrew Lang, and Tim Perry.

Barkley's time with the Sixers was less successful for the team than the decade that came before it, but things would get much worse, and rapidly, after Barkley left. In eight years in Philadelphia, Barkley went to the conference finals once and the conference semifinals three times. In the five years that followed the trade, the Sixers never won more than 26 games, and they wouldn't make the playoffs again until their next home run lottery pick, Allen Iverson, reached his prime.

Barkley's move to Phoenix was immediately successful, as Barkley was surrounded by better supporting players than he'd had since he himself was one of Moses Malone's supporting players. Under rookie head coach Paul Westphal, seven Suns averaged double figures in scoring as Phoenix led the NBA in points per game and offensive efficiency. The fast-paced Suns took more three-pointers than any other team in the NBA—led by Dan Majerle and Danny Ainge, as well as Barkley, who chucked a career-high 220 threes—and made the third-highest percentage.

Phoenix won 62 games and cakewalked to a seven-game division title win as Barkley, who averaged 25.6 points, 12.2 rebounds, and a career-high 5.1 assists per game, took home MVP honors with 59 out of 98 first-place votes.

In the playoffs, the Suns very nearly became the first No. 1 seed to lose in the first round, dropping the first two games to a Lakers team that had been denuded of Magic, Kareem, Worthy, and the rest of the mainstays of the Showtime teams. Barkley and the Suns came back to win three straight to take the series, then knocked off David Robinson and the Spurs in six games.

In the conference finals, Barkley's Suns faced a young Seattle Supersonics team that was breaking in its own boards-crashing monster power forward, Shawn Kemp. Over seven games, Barkley outrebounded Kemp 97-65 and scored a series-leading 179 points to lead the Suns past Seattle 4-3.

In the NBA Finals, Barkley and Jordan conducted a legendary one-on-one battle, with Jordan emerging victorious.

"I never walked onto a basketball court when I didn't feel like I was as good as anyone else out there. Except once. Game

2 of the 1993 NBA Finals in Chicago," Barkley later told *Sports Illustrated*'s Jack McCallum. "We had lost Game 1, and I had made up my mind that I would do anything—anything—to lead my team in Game 2. I scored 42 points and Michael simply would not let me win. I looked over at him and thought, *Man, he's better than me. He's better than everybody.* Trust me on this: Nobody has ever played basketball like Michael."

Barkley scored 42 points and pulled down 13 rebounds, while Jordan went for 42 points, 12 rebounds, and nine assists in a three-point Chicago win. Game 3 in Phoenix went to three overtimes, and Jordan dropped another 44 points, while Barkley battled foul trouble and still contributed 24 points, 19 rebounds, and 53 minutes in an eight-point Suns win. In Game 4, Barkley dropped a triple-double, but Jordan scored 55 and the Bulls won by six in Phoenix. The Suns stole game 5 in Chicago, then staged a furious fourth-quarter comeback in Game 6, thanks to 21 points and 17 boards by Barkley, but their effort came up one point short. John Paxson scored the go-ahead three-pointer with 3.9 seconds left—the only three of Chicago's 12 fourth-quarter points to come from anyone other than Jordan—before Kevin Johnson had his buzzer-beater attempt blocked. Barkley never came that close to winning a title again.

Barkley, who turned 30 that winter, started to feel the effects of age. Barkley missed 17 games due to injuries and shot below 50 percent from the floor for the first time in his career, but he and his team were nearly as successful. In 1993–94, the Suns won 56 games, again, behind the NBA's highest-scoring offense, with Barkley chipping in a team-high 21.6 points and 11.6 rebounds per game. The next season, the Suns won 59 games and the division, with the team finishing second in points and third in points per possession, thanks in part to Barkley's 23 points and 11.1 rebounds. Both seasons, the Suns followed up an opening-round sweep with a seven-game loss to the eventual NBA champion Rockets.

After the 1995–96 season, which the Suns finished 41-41 despite Barkley's 22.6 points and 11.2 rebounds per game, the 33-year-old Barkley was once again named to the Olympic team, once again won gold, and was once again traded, this time to the Rockets team that had crushed his playoff dreams in 1994 and 1995.

The 1996–97 Rockets won 57 games and finished in the top 10 in both offensive and defensive efficiency, but they would've been a much better team in 1987. Five of their top six players in minutes played—Barkley, Olajuwon, Clyde Drexler, Kevin Willis, and Mario Elie—were 33 years old or older, which isn't awesome if you're putting together a Ryder Cup team, much less an NBA team.

For his part, Barkley found himself playing second chair for the first time since Moses Malone left Philadelphia. Barkley played fewer games than any other season in his career, and took fewer shots per minute than he had in any season since 1986–87. Barkley made his last All-Star team anyway, thanks not only to his reputation, but to his 19.5 points and 13.5 re-bounds per game. The Rockets lost in the Western Conference finals to the Utah Jazz. In 1997–98, Barkley and Olajuwon both missed significant time and the Rockets dropped to 41-41 after not changing their aging core, and earned another playoff loss to the Finals-bound Jazz.

The next year, the Rockets ditched Elie and Willis, and Drexler retired. To replace them, Houston brought in another aging superstar, Scottie Pippen, and rookie Cuttino Mobley. They rebounded to 31-19 in a lockout-shortened season, but ran into another burgeoning dynasty, the Shaq-and-Kobe-led Los Angeles Lakers, and lost 3-1 in the first round. Barkley had a team-high 20 points and six assists in the Game 4 loss, his final playoff game.

The next year, Barkley played only 18 games, the 17th of which came against the Sixers in Philadelphia. Barkley played eight minutes and tore a tendon in his leg, which sidelined him for four months. It was the only game of Barkley's career in which he didn't score at least one point. Rather than retire, Barkley rehabbed the injury and returned to play one last game in April of that year before retiring at the age of thirty-six.

Because so many of Barkley's career highlights came in a Suns uniform or in a Team USA uniform or in *Space Jam*, it sometimes doesn't seem like he belonged to Philadelphia the way Dr. J or Iverson did. Barkley himself told McCallum: "If I'm lucky enough to go into the Hall of Fame, I'll go in as a Philadelphia 76er. I don't think I was always treated well there, but you should go into the Hall with the team you had your best years on, even though I was the MVP in Phoenix."

He did just that in 2006.

Barkley toyed with a political career, publicly contemplating running for governor of his native Alabama, before giving that up for a second career as an analyst on TNT's "Inside the NBA."

One of the game's most efficient scorers and most persistent offensive rebounders, Barkley is sixth in NBA history in offensive rebounds, eighth all-time in true shooting percentage, and 11th all-time in free throw attempts. As a fan, what you want out of a player is for him to be good or, failing that, be entertaining. Barkley, as an entire package, was an unmatched combination of the two.

REGGIE WHITE

14 After almost 25 years of being defined by pass-heavy offensive innovation, the Eagles are still living in the shadow of Reggie White. White was not only a spectacular player in his own right, but the teams he played on, through their style and personality, also invited that kind of trans-generational devotion.

There's a concept in popular culture called fan service, in which the creators of some narrative fiction—television shows, comic books, etc.—add an element to their product for no other purpose than to make their fans happy. It's called "fan service," and it's exactly what it sounds like. Fan service has its origins in Japanese anime, and in that context, it usually involves showcasing more attractive female characters in various states of undress. Not enough to be pornographic, but enough to titillate the audience.

Buddy Ryan was fan service for the Philadelphia Eagles. He was widely revered as a defensive genius, inventor of the fearsome 46 that helped the Chicago Bears to a 15-1 season and a Super Bowl in 1985–86. Ryan's defenses were fast, aggressive, and overwhelmingly successful, not unlike those of his son Rex, now head coach of the New York Jets. Like Rex,

Buddy was brash, candid, and confident, which endeared him to Philadelphia fans. Unlike Rex, Buddy was also coarse and quick to anger, which endeared him to Philadelphia fans even more. As defensive coordinator of the Houston Oilers, the sixty-two-year-old Ryan punched fellow assistant coach Kevin Gilbride on the sidelines during a game. Ryan allegedly placed bounties on Cowboys players and encouraged his own players to fight each other in training camp.

Said former Deadspin and Gawker editor-in-chief (and Eagles fan) A.J. Daulerio: "Buddy Ryan was a walking, talking version of the mythology Philadelphia fans idolize about themselves."

It's true: the identity Eagles fans relish is grounded in Buddy Ryan, not the more successful, more calm, offensive-minded Dick Vermeil and Andy Reid.

Ryan's defenses were exactly what fans wanted to see: skilled, aggressive, brash, and impenetrable. Ryan lined up big, strong guys, told them to kill the man with the ball, and minted stars: Seth Joyner, Andre Waters, Eric Allen, Clyde Simmons, Byron Evans, Jerome Brown, and Reggie White.

They were known as Gang Green, which conjures up images not only of high-quality punmaking, but also of a kind of insidious, dangerous nastiness, the kind of image that defensive linemen take particular joy in cultivating.

The best player on Gang Green was White, a six-foot-five 300-pound defensive end who was, at the time, the best defensive player in Eagles history, and there's a solid argument for taking away at least one of those qualifiers: "defensive" or

"Eagles." White was the perfect defensive end for his era. Today's top pass rushers get by primarily based on speed—sometime in the mid-1990s, colleges began to pump out six-foot-seven 340-pound monsters with 37-inch arms and the quickness and athleticism of an NBA forward. As offensive tackles turned into mountains that could move, it became apparent that the best way to get past an offensive tack was to go around, not through him. So edge rushers started to get smaller and quicker—White would have dwarfed a 21st century pass rusher like Jared Allen, Von Miller, or DeMarcus Ware, all players who were better-adapted to pure speed rushing and to counter not only the shotgun spread, but nowadays, the read option as well.

To say that this wasn't White's game might sell him short on the surface, because he was plenty fast and plenty athletic, but he was more of a power rusher and all-around player, more akin to someone like J.J. Watt and better suited to offenses that operated mostly with the quarterback under center and were less subtle than the offenses of today.

White's signature move involved exploding up into the tackle at the snap, extending his arms and driving with his legs to push him back, then crossing inside to attack the quarterback. The end result was a combination of sumo wrestling and basketball that took advantage of White's incredible strength and quickness.

Larry Allen is a Hall of Fame offensive guard who played for the Cowboys and 49ers. He made the Pro Bowl in 11 of his 14 seasons in the league. But in 1994, he was a rookie, pressed into the Cowboys' starting lineup by injuries, and he found himself facing White and the Green Bay Packers.

On the first play from scrimmage, White used this move to knock the 325-pound Allen flat on his back en route to sacking quarterback Jason Garrett.

"One second I was blocking him," Allen told Ray Didinger of the *Daily News*, "the next second, I was flying through the air, thinking, *What is this?* I never had that feeling before."

There must have been a time before Reggie White was a great defensive end, but it doesn't exist in any sort of public memory. White was born December 19, 1961 in Chattanooga, Tennessee, and lived there throughout his childhood, which culminated in a 140-tackle senior season that earned him All-America honors and the distinction of being named the top high school recruit in the state. White, who had also lettered in basketball, was only listed at 238 pounds as a college freshman, but he'd grow into an All-America defensive tackle at the University of Tennessee.

White broke into the Volunteers' starting lineup midway through his freshman year and stayed there through a remarkable senior season: 72 solo tackles, 15 sacks, 9 tackles for loss, and a Citrus Bowl win over Maryland that involved White knocking Boomer Esiason out of the game. After that season, White, perhaps on a personal quest to move methodically westward across the state of Tennessee, terrorizing offensive linemen as he went, signed with the Memphis Showboats of the USFL, the outlaw spring football league. White played two largely successful seasons with Memphis before the league folded, leaving him to join the Philadelphia Eagles.

The Eagles took White fourth overall in the 1984 Supplemental Draft, and 18 months later, they got a fully-formed veteran.

In 1985, the Eagles were in the midst of a near-decade-long hangover after their run to Super Bowl XV, and while they went 7-9 in 1985 and fired coach Marion Campbell, the Eagles introduced arguably the two most important players of the Buddy Ryan era: White and Randall Cunningham, a 1985 second-round pick out of UNLV.

White played 13 games as an NFL rookie, starting 12. He made the most of them, recording 100 tackles, 13 sacks, and two fumble recoveries. White didn't make the Pro Bowl that year, but he'd make up for it in every single one of the next 13 seasons.

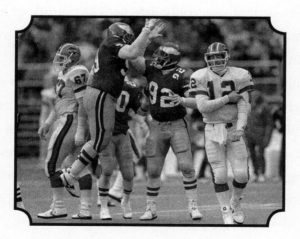

Reggie White *(AP Photo/Charles Krupa)*

In 1986, Ryan, fresh off the Super Bowl, set out to revitalize the Eagles's defense. Ryan, along with defensive assistants Wade

Phillips and Jeff Fisher, changed the Eagles's scheme from a 3-4 to a 4-3, and White, who had played end in the 3-4 under Campbell, remained inside for part of the 1986 season before switching to defensive end for good. Ryan's first season in charge was rocky—the Eagles went 5-10-1 as they switched quarterbacks from Ron Jaworski to Cunningham, but White recorded 98 tackles and 18 sacks.

Though White was already an All-Pro in 1986, he stepped up his game to a new level in 1987. Despite only playing in 12 games, he recorded at least one sack in 11 of them and at least two in eight games to finish the season with 21, a league-leading total as well as an Eagles team record, and one of only nine 20-sack seasons in NFL history. White also scored his first career touchdown, scooping up a fumble and running it back 70 yards in a 34-24 loss to Washington on September 13. For his efforts, White was named the NFL's defensive player of the year.

White led the NFL in sacks again the next season with 18, and for the first time in his career, made the playoffs. After winning the NFC East, White's Eagles were rewarded with a December 31 game against the Bears at Soldier Field, which turned out to be one of the more bizarre playoff spectacles in league history. In the middle of the second quarter, a thick fog rolled in off Lake Michigan, reducing visibility to about 10-15 yards. Cunningham, who passed 54 times anyway, couldn't see his receivers, nor could broadcasters Verne Lundquist and Terry Bradshaw see the field. The Eagles were never able to generate much offense, and in spite of a sack by White, lost the Fog Bowl 20-12.

The next two seasons were the same: Pro Bowl and All-Pro honors for White and a Wild Card berth and a first-round exit for the Eagles, after which the team, fed up with Ryan, who'd gone 0-for-3 in playoff games, fired him and promoted offensive coordinator Rich Kotite.

The 1991 season was a missed opportunity for the Eagles—White anchored a truly spectacular defense, recording 100 tackles and 15 sacks, while the team finished fifth in scoring defense, fourth in total defense, and second in yards allowed per play, and the 244 points the Eagles allowed in 1991 would be the lowest total in his Eagles tenure.

However, Cunningham blew out his knee after only four pass attempts and backup Jim McMahon couldn't adequately replace him. The Eagles scored 111 fewer points in 1991 than they did in 1990, and they missed the playoffs in an extremely competitive NFC, despite winning 10 games.

Kotite managed to win 11 games in 1992 and the Eagles returned to the playoffs, and for the first time since their Super Bowl year, managed to win a game before being knocked out by the eventual champion Cowboys in the divisional round. The 34-10 loss in Dallas would be White's last game in an Eagles uniform.

As great as White's on-the-field achievements were, his involvement in the creation of free agency might be his most enduring legacy. The 1970s and 1980s were periods of great labor unrest across all North American sports, as players for the first time began to seek out a degree of self-determination.

Though the NFL allowed limited free agency beginning in 1977, by 1989, the players had staged two unsuccessful strikes that, despite wiping games off the schedule, won them next to nothing in terms of concessions.

In 1989, the NFLPA decertified, allowing individual players to sue the NFL. A series of victories in antitrust suits led to White filing a class-action suit against the league in 1993. At that point, the NFL settled White's suit, set out to negotiate a new collective bargaining agreement and allowed free agency in exchange for a salary cap.

White was one of the first high-profile players to exercise his newfound freedom, signing a four-year, $17 million contract with the Green Bay Packers that nearly tripled his salary and made him the third-highest player in the NFL.

White, thirty-two, came to Green Bay at the right time: the year before, the Packers had hired Bill Walsh protégé Mike Holmgren as head coach and installed Brett Favre at quarterback. In 1993, White's first year, they made the playoffs for the first time since 1982—and would do so in the next six consecutive years, until Holmgren and White left the team after the 1998 season. White recorded 13 sacks for a team that hadn't had a defensive lineman record more than five sacks since 1985.

White also carried over his rivalry with Cowboys linemen to Green Bay—Dallas ended White's season every year dating back to 1992, and Larry Allen and Erik Williams became some of White's most formidable adversaries. However, in 1996, the Packers finally got over the hump, winning 13 games in the regular season and three more in the playoffs to give White, who had just turned thirty-six, his first and only Super Bowl title.

White, keenly aware of the stage on which he found himself, had the best game of his playoff career: a Super Bowl record three sacks as the Packers held the Patriots to 257 total yards and forced Drew Bledsoe to throw four interceptions.

Green Bay returned to the Super Bowl the next year, but lost to the Denver Broncos, and in 1998, White, then 37 years old, had his last great season: 16 sacks earned him defensive player of the year honors for the second time in his career, and for the last time, Pro Bowl and All-Pro honors.

White announced his retirement after the 1998 season, but came back after a year off to play one season for the Carolina Panthers. After the 2000 season, he hung up his spikes for good.

White, who had been an ordained Baptist minister and committed evangelist throughout his career, and his public enthusiasm for his faith had led to his being christened "Minister of Defense," returned his focus to these religious practices. His post-career ministry was cut short, however, when on December 26, 2004, he suffered a fatal cardiac arrhythmia, believed to have been brought on by sarcoidosis and sleep apnea, two disorders from which White had suffered for years. He was forty-three years old.

White rewrote the NFL record book for defensive linemen: his 198 career sacks was an NFL record at the time he retired, as were his 13 consecutive Pro Bowl selections and nine consecutive seasons with 10 or more sacks. White recorded 124 sacks in only 121 games for the Eagles, still a franchise record, and his 68.5 sacks for the Packers were a franchise record at the time of his retirement, though he was later passed by Kabeer Gbaja-Biamila. White was named to the NFL's 75th Anniversary team and All-Decade teams for the 1980s and 1990s. He was elected to the College Football Hall of Fame in 2002, and in 2005, the Packers, Eagles, and Tennessee Volunteers all retired White's No. 92. On August 5, 2006, White's wife and son accepted his posthumous enshrinement into the Pro Football Hall of Fame.

STEVE CARLTON

15 If Steve Carlton had been born five or 10 years later, he probably wouldn't have come to Philadelphia. Carlton is unquestionably of the Phillies—he played fifteen years in Philadelphia, more than any other pitcher. Among Phillies, Carlton has the most wins and strikeouts, pitched the second-most innings, and is the live ball era leader in shutouts. The Phillies retired his No. 32 and in 1994, he became the franchise's first first-ballot Hall of Famer.

But unlike Robin Roberts, Cole Hamels, Curt Schilling, and some of the franchise's other great starting pitchers, Carlton didn't arrive in the organization as an amateur, or as a failed prospect in need of redemption—he was the genuine article from day one, a fully-formed top-of-the-rotation pitcher with three All-Star games and a World Series ring under his belt. He didn't find success in Philadelphia so much as he brought success with him.

Carlton was born on December 22, 1944 in Miami, Florida, where he lived for his entire childhood, up to and including college, where he briefly attended Miami Dade Community

College before signing with the St. Louis Cardinals in 1963 for $5,000. Carlton made only 27 appearances in the minors as a nineteen-year-old before being called up in April 1965. He pitched intermittently in relief for two years before finally breaking into the rotation in 1967, when he went 14-9 with a 2.98 ERA in 30 appearances (28 starts) for the eventual World Series winners. Carlton, then twenty-two, found himself serving an apprenticeship on a Cardinals team full of now-familiar names. Four members of that team—Carlton, Bob Gibson, Lou Brock, and Orlando Cepeda—would go on to make the Hall of Fame.

That team also featured catcher Tim McCarver, whose partnership with Carlton would be so significant to both of their careers that McCarver once said, "When Steve and I die, we are going to be buried 60 feet, 6 inches apart."

In 1967, Carlton made only one World Series start, a six-inning, five-strikeout Game 5 performance in which he surrendered only one unearned run. However, the Cardinals managed only a single ninth-inning consolation run against Carlton's future Phillies teammate Jim Lonborg, the American League Cy Young winner, and Carlton took the loss.

The next year, Gibson was the undisputed ace of the staff. In 1967, Gibson missed time after a Roberto Clemente line drive broke his leg, though Gibson came back to win three games and hit a home run against the Red Sox in the World Series. In 1968, Gibson was completely healthy and put up one of the more remarkable seasons in recent history: a 1.12 ERA, 13 shutouts, 268 strikeouts, and only 5.8 hits per nine innings, all league-leading totals. Though it speaks volumes about the run-scoring environment that with a 1.12 ERA and a 97-win team behind him, Gibson only went 22-9.

Carlton wasn't nearly that good—his 2.99 ERA looks good now, but adjusting for ballpark and league average, it was fairly pedestrian. Carlton didn't make a start in the 1968 World Series, appearing twice for mopup duty in blowout losses—and the Cardinals lost to the Tigers in seven games. But while playing exhibition games in Japan that offseason, Carlton started to tinker with a slider, a pitch that would develop into not only his most effective weapon, but also pretty much anyone's most effective weapon.

In 1969, Carlton came into his own—a 6.8 WAR season where he more or less matched Gibson's performance on a rate basis, though Gibson threw more innings. On September 15, Carlton tied a major league record by striking out 19 batters in a nine-inning game, a 4-3 loss to the Mets, and denied himself a chance at 20 by picking Bud Harrelson off at first in the ninth inning. 1970 and 1971 were a little less productive for Carlton, and his salary demands stopped being palatable for Cardinals owner Gussie Busch. The two sides were between $5,000 and $10,000 apart, and in the reserve clause era, Carlton had to choose between re-signing with St. Louis and not playing at all. The standoff ended on February 25, 1972, when the Cardinals agreed to swap unhappy starting pitchers with the Phillies, sending Carlton to Philadelphia for Rick Wise.

You could say that 1972 was Carlton's breakout season. More on what, exactly, he did in a moment, but with a pitcher as great as Carlton, it's both entertaining and instructive to figure out how he did it.

For starters, Carlton was a superb athlete with a backbreaking work ethic. When most people talk about athleticism, they mean running fast and being able to do bench presses, but there's more to athleticism than that, particularly for pitchers. Athleticism includes reflexes, agility, flexibility, developing muscle memory, and fluidity of motion. Everyone likes to talk about Greg Maddux having been a great pitcher in spite of his lack of athleticism—this is an easy narrative because Maddux looks less like a professional athlete than he looks like the guy who taught the professional athlete's eighth-grade Spanish class. But it's so entirely wrong.

Maddux was an unbelievable athlete, light on his feet and in total control of his body, in spite of not being particularly tall or fast or muscular. He was extremely durable at a position that eats more imposing ballplayers alive. Carlton had that Greg Maddux-type athleticism—the body control, the flexibility, the ability to repeat his delivery, in the archetypal power pitcher's body. For someone as big as Carlton to fold up, lean back, turn, and hide the ball from the batter the way he did takes tremendous flexibility and balance, and he repeated his delivery well, which is difficult for a pitcher with as involved a windup as Carlton had.

All of this is not to say that Carlton wasn't athletic in the traditional sense. In his 2001 *New Historical Baseball Abstract*, Bill James ranked Carlton as the 15th-best pitcher of all time, saying this:

> "Carlton was the hardest working, best-conditioned baseball player of his generation, as strong as an NFL linebacker. He used to climb into a vat of dry rice, and exercise by jogging 20 minutes buried in dry rice. Every step was like a marathon."

Carlton could also help himself with the bat: he hit .201 / .223 / .259 for his career, with 13 home runs, four of which came in games where he also registered a complete game shutout.

Carlton's greatest weapon, the slider, entered the picture during an exhibition series in Japan after the 1968 season. Carlton said he began tinkering with it after giving up a home run to Sadaharu Oh. When Oh faced him again, Carlton threw it at the Japanese home run king's ribs, causing Oh to duck out of the way, and it broke back over the plate for a strike.

That slider, slow and late-moving with a sharp two-plane break, went on to become Carlton's signature pitch, and the foundation for a 1972 that would go down as one of the greatest pitching performances in the modern game.

Steve Carlton *(AP Photo/Rusty Kennedy)*

Rick Wise, by the way, was pretty good for St. Louis in 1972: 269 innings, 110 ERA+, 142 strikeouts and 4.9 WAR. Carlton was better.

The thing about 1972 that everyone gets hung up on is that Carlton won 27 games for a team that only won 59. That's pretty astounding, but from a standpoint of statistics, we can do better.

Carlton's ERA+ in 1972 was 182, the 50th-best mark in the expansion era, which is pretty impressive: adjusting for league and stadium effects, Carlton's 1972 was one of the best in the past 50 years on a rate basis. Batters hit .207/.257/.291 off Carlton that year—Carlton himself hit .197/.236/.265.

But Carlton wasn't just great on a rate basis—he performed in quantity as well as quality: Carlton made 41 starts and finished 30 of them for a total of 346 1/3 innings, the fourth-highest total in the expansion era, and an even more impressive total when you consider Carlton lost at least one start, perhaps more, to a player strike that claimed the first week of the season. On a per-inning basis, he gave up fewer hits than anyone in the National League, except Don Sutton. But he threw so many innings that he led the National League in total hits allowed.

Carlton struck out 310 batters—roughly three and a half times as many as he walked. It was Carlton's only 300-strikeout season and one of only 28 such seasons by any pitcher in the expansion era.

When all was said and done, Carlton had accumulated 12.1 wins above replacement, tied with Doc Gooden in 1985 for the best season by any starting pitcher in the expansion era. Carlton led the National League in, among other things, wins, starts, complete games, ERA, strikeouts, K/BB ratio, and batters faced. It was a tremendous season and an unbelievably good introduction to Philadelphia. Carlton won the Cy Young unanimously.

Carlton earned himself a $100,000 raise and came back to lead the league in innings pitched again the next year, but those innings were somewhat less effective—Carlton more than doubled his ERA and went from being a 12-win player to a 2-win player.

Among Carlton's more unbelievable achievements is that he did not speak to the media for the last 15 years of his career. Carlton's drop-off from his historic 1972 to a pedestrian 1973 created a to-do, as is common in Philadelphia sports media, and by the end of 1973, Carlton figured it was just not worth the trouble to talk to the press, and he never again spoke to the press until he retired.

"I was tired of getting slammed," Carlton said after his retirement. "To me it was a slap in the face. But it made me concentrate better. And the irony is that they wrote better without access to my quotes. It's all quotes, anyway, and it all sounds the same to me. After that they wrote better and more interesting stuff. I took it personal. I got slammed quite a bit. To pick up the paper and read about yourself getting slammed, that doesn't start your day off right."

The Phillies, however, began laying the groundwork for their first sustained run of success in almost 100 years. In addition to Carlton, Greg Luzinski took over the left field role full-time in 1972. In 1973, Mike Schmidt played his first full season in the major leagues (he was terrible, but he didn't stay that way for long), and the team won 12 more games in 1973 than they had the year before, despite Carlton's regression.

Carlton bounced back in 1974 to make the All-Star team as the Phillies improved by nine more games. They made it over .500 in 1975, and in 1976, it all came together: 101 wins, a franchise record, and a roster that started to resemble the eventual 1980 World Champions.

The Phillies' first division title pitted them against the Big Red Machine in the NLCS, and the Phillies' first playoff appearance since 1950 . . . well, it went badly.

Carlton gave up five runs in seven innings in Game 1—the first-ever playoff game at Veterans Stadium—and took the loss. In Game 2, Jim Lonborg walked Ken Griffey in the first inning, then didn't allow another baserunner until the sixth inning, but three of the four batters he faced in that inning reached base and scored.

The Phillies led Game 3 in the ninth inning, but Ron Reed, Gene Garber, and Tom Underwood recorded only one out between them, but managed to allow three runs, including a series-ending RBI single by Ken Griffey.

1977 was a little better to Carlton—now thirty-two years old, he posted a 5.9 WAR season, with a 2.64 ERA and 198 strikeouts in 283 innings, a performance that was good enough for Carlton's second Cy Young Award. The Phillies again won 101 games, but again, Carlton and his teammates got beaten up in the NLCS, losing to the Dodgers 3-1 as Carlton took a no decision in Game 1 after surrendering five runs in 6 ⅔ innings, and the loss in Game 4.

In 1978, Carlton posted similar rate stats, but threw about 40 fewer innings and won seven fewer games. The Phillies won the division again and once again lost to the Dodgers in a four-game NLCS, though Carlton won Game 3, a complete-game, four-run effort that marked the first postseason victory for Carlton in 11 years. This season marked three consecutive postseason appearances for the Phillies after having made the playoffs twice before in franchise history.

Carlton's 1980 would have been the best season of just about anyone else's career. It was the poor man's version of 1972: league-leading totals in wins, ERA+, starts, innings pitched, batters faced, and K/BB ratio, this time earning Carlton 10.2 WAR. A single vote for Jerry Reuss of the Dodgers kept Carlton's third Cy Young from being unanimous as well. Schmidt was the unanimous MVP, and Lonnie Smith finished third in Rookie of the Year voting with a .339/.397/.443 line with 33 steals as a fourth out-fielder, bringing the Phillies as close as they've ever come to a clean sweep of the league's major awards.

The Phillies, who had brought in first baseman Pete Rose and moved Dallas Green from the front office to the manager's role the season before, won 92 games and the division. For the first time since 1967, Carlton stood out in the play-offs—he allowed only one run in seven innings in Game 1 of a nerve-racking five-game NLCS against the Astros, and won both of his World Series starts against Kansas City.

Carlton's second World Series start, a seven-inning, one-run, seven-strikeout effort, was particularly significant, as it clinched the first championship in franchise history.

Carlton managed to defy aging trends and have his best three-year stretch in his late thirties, from 1980–82. Carlton finished third in Cy Young voting in a 1981 season that was divided by a strike halfway through. Rather than crown a single winner in each division in the strike-shortened season, MLB had the team with the best record in the first half of the season play the team with the best record in the second half. This was the first divisional playoff round in baseball history, and the only one until the idea became a permanent fixture starting in 1995.

The first-half champion Phillies played the second-half champion Montreal Expos in the NLDS, and while Carlton pitched well, he lost both of his starts to Montreal ace Steve Rogers, who allowed a single run in 17 ⅔ innings to lead the Expos past the Phillies in five games.

Carlton tossed more or less identical seasons in 1982 and 1983. He tallied 295 ⅔ innings, 286 strikeouts (both league-leading totals), 119 ERA+, and 5.5 WAR in 1982. In 1983, Carlton again led the league in innings pitched with 283 ⅔, and in strikeouts with 275, 116 ERA+, and 5.5 WAR. Of course, Carlton went 23-11 in 1982 and won his then-record fourth and final Cy Young Award, while in 2013, Carlton went 15-16 and didn't get a single vote as teammate John Denny won the Cy Young.

In 1983, the Phillies, having cobbled together a collection of veterans of the 1980 World Series team and Big Red Machine veterans, made the playoffs for the last time in Carlton's career, and in 1983, Carlton arguably had his best-ever playoffs: a combined one run allowed in 13 ⅔ NLCS innings against Los Angeles and a respectable losing effort against Jim Palmer in Game 3 of the World Series.

In addition to his last postseason start, Carlton registered a couple other notable milestones in 1983. At age thirty-nine, Carlton registered his 300th career win, a 6-2 victory over the Giants on September 23. That same season, Carlton, Nolan Ryan, and Gaylord Perry all surpassed Walter Johnson's career strikeout record. Ryan was first, but the lead changed hands among the three of them throughout 1983 and 1984. Carlton last held the record in September 1984, after which Ryan passed him for good.

After 1984, the forty-year-old Carlton, one of the most effective and durable pitchers of the previous two decades, finally gave in to age. In 1985, Carlton threw only 92 innings as injuries began to slow him down, and he started 1986 with a 6.18 ERA in 16 starts. On June 24, the Phillies released the most decorated pitcher in franchise history.

Carlton would spend the next two and a half seasons bouncing from team to team, spending a month with the Giants in 1986 and becoming the second pitcher, after Ryan, to strike out 4,000 batters in a career. After the Giants released him, Carlton signed with the Chicago White Sox, then the Cleveland Indians, who traded him to the Minnesota Twins at the 1987 deadline. Carlton would earn a third World Series title with Minnesota, though he made only nine appearances and posted a 6.70 ERA, and he did not pitch in the postseason.

On April 23, 1988, the 43-year-old Carlton allowed nine runs in a five-inning start against the Cleveland Indians. The Twins released him before his next start and he never pitched in the majors again, capping a career that spanned 24 seasons, included 329 wins, 4,136 strikeouts, and 84 wins above replacement, (second among expansion-era lefthanders to Randy Johnson), and an all-time record 144 pickoffs. He was inducted to the Hall of Fame in 1994.

BRIAN DAWKINS

16 Brian Dawkins is my favorite NFL player ever. I imagine I have that in common with about 80 percent of Eagles fans who are old enough to remember the entire Andy Reid era, but not old enough to remember the Buddy Ryan era.

Dawkins was a foundational player in the most successful era of Eagles football, by all accounts the emotional leader of the defense, and an inescapable force on the field. Dawkins had a reputation as a hard hitter, but, the Ike Hilliard hit notwithstanding, Dawkins wouldn't be going to the Hall of Fame if his ability to lay out receivers was the only thing he had going for him—he wasn't Ronnie Lott or Steve Atwater. That's not to say that Dawkins was a bad tackler or wasn't capable of delivering the occasional highlight reel hit, because he was. It just wasn't what set him apart.

Neither was Dawkins in the Ed Reed mold of free safety. Dawkins was an expert ballhawk—he intercepted 37 passes in his career, 34 of them with the Eagles, which ties him for the most in franchise history. But Reed and safeties like him are often described as center fielders, which is a bit of crossover sports jargon I love because of how descriptive it is. A great ballhawking safety is like a center fielder—if the quarterback throws a deep ball anywhere near him, he'll read it, track it down, and make a play on it. Dawkins was good in coverage, but Ed Reed's game wasn't his game.

Two things set Dawkins apart from his contemporaries: the first was his ubiquity. Dawkins was the anchor of one of the best defensive backfields in football for more than a decade, and it's not like he just sat back 20 yards from the line of scrimmage and waited for a post route to jump. Dawkins was helping his corners on deep routes, sneaking up to the line of scrimmage in run support, covering tight ends and running backs one-on-one when necessary, and, from time to time, spying on more run-happy quarterbacks like Michael Vick. The easiest way to find Dawkins on a football field was to look for the ball.

Dawkins played safety like he knew the cheat codes.

The second defining characteristic of Dawkins was the panache with which he played the game. Dawkins was listed at six feet, 210 pounds, which isn't really all that big for a normal person, let alone a football player. But in uniform, Dawkins looked like a cartoon character, with bulging muscles in his arms and that signature blacked-out visor. In fact, enough people called him Weapon X, in reference to the X-Men character, that Marvel honored Dawkins with a custom poster when he retired. Dawkins has Wolverine-like claws in the poster, but other than that, the legendary comic book studio didn't exaggerate his appearance at all. And at any rate, how sure *can* we be that Dawkins's bones aren't made of adamantium, anyway?

If Dawkins is a mutant, he's done a good job of hiding it. Dawkins was born on October 13, 1973 in Jacksonville, Florida. Dawkins first came to prominence while attending William M. Raines High School in Jacksonville, a school that's been quite good to the Philadelphia Eagles over the years: in addition to Dawkins, Raines produced fellow Pro Bowl defensive back Lito Sheppard and receiver Harold Carmichael, the Eagles' all-time leader, by far, in receptions, receiving yards, and receiving touchdowns.

Dawkins went on to play four years at Clemson University in South Carolina, where he enjoyed a decorated, if not record-breaking, career. Dawkins was a three-time All-ACC player with the Tigers, and as a senior, he made the AP All-America Team after leading the conference in interceptions. Of the four Eagles in this book, Dawkins probably had the least impressive collegiate career.

Dawkins did enough at Clemson to catch the attention of the Philadelphia Eagles, who picked him in the second round, No. 61 overall, in the 1996 NFL draft.

Dawkins stepped into the lineup immediately, starting 13 games in an effective safety battery with veteran Michael Zordich. Dawkins finished tied for second on the team with three interceptions and finished tied for fourth on the team with 53 tackles as the Eagles went 10-6, but suffered a demoralizing 14-0 Wild Card loss to San Francisco.

Things went downhill rapidly after that. The Eagles went 6-9-1 the next year, then 3-13 the year after that. The only consolation from those years is that they set the stage for what was to come. In 1995, the Eagles spent a second-round pick on cornerback Bobby Taylor, and the next year, in addition to Dawkins, acquired Troy Vincent, giving them three starters in the defensive backfield who were twenty-five or younger in 1996. Those three would mature through the late 1990s into one of the best units in the game. Over the next three seasons, the Eagles drafted Duce Staley, Tra (later William) Thomas, Jeremiah Trotter, Al Harris, and Donovan McNabb, essentially the core of the team that would more or less dominate the NFC East in the 2000s. Perhaps most importantly, they fired head coach Ray Rhodes in 1999—because almost no NFL head coach survives a 3-13 season—and replaced him with a relative unknown: a laconic forty-year-old named Andy Reid, the Green Bay Packers' quarterbacks coach. Reid, a passing game specialist, hired another relative unknown to run the defense: Seahawks linebackers coach Jim Johnson.

Head coaches often become inextricably tied to their quarterbacks, particularly when they are together as long as Reid and McNabb, who share so much success, and are criticized for so many of the same reasons.

But on the other side of the ball, Johnson and Dawkins forged a similar relationship. In style, Johnson was the spiritual successor to Buddy Ryan, an aggressive playcaller who loved the blitz, as well as skilled defensive backs and small, athletic defenders. It was under Johnson that Dawkins went from being good to being legendary.

Dawkins's intelligence, versatility, and almost suicidal aggressiveness made him the perfect weapon for Johnson, who employed his star free safety closer to the box, almost as a fourth linebacker at times. Johnson worked with Dawkins the way Michelangelo worked in marble, and both achieved tremendous success as a result.

"They were a match made in heaven," said former Eagles linebacker Ike Reese. "I don't know that Brian goes on to become the Hall of Fame safety that he was without Jim Johnson." Reese said that one of the highlights of the week was attending defensive meetings in which Johnson would hand out new plays and schemes for the coming game, and as often as not, the focal point of those plays was Dawkins.

When Dawkins returned to Philadelphia to announce his retirement, Johnson's was the first name Dawkins mentioned in his speech, and the nine-time Pro Bowler broke down in tears immediately.

"Jim saw something in me," Dawkins said, "and he began to use me in a different way than a lot of safeties were being used at the time. He believed in me . . . The reason I made so many plays in crunch time was that Jim continued to call my number in crunch time. He knew I would do whatever it took. He knew I would give up a body part if I had to, to make sure his blitzes went home."

Dawkins' first season under Reid and Johnson was better for him than it was for the rest of the team: Dawkins set new career highs with four interceptions and six forced fumbles, while the Eagles went 5-11 while struggling to generate any offense whatsoever, and that record was inflated by a Week 17 win over the eventual Super Bowl champion St. Louis Rams, who had already clinched home-field advantage and pulled their starters in the second half. But Dawkins, 26, made his first Pro Bowl and established himself as the cornerstone of a defense that would improve rapidly in the years to come.

It was the next season, 2000, when the Eagles started to put it all together. McNabb took over as the Eagles' full-time starter, and led a team to the playoffs that had no business being there. After a 200-yard rushing performance on Opening Day in what came to be known as the Pickle Juice Game, Duce Staley went down after five games with a Lisfranc fracture in his foot, leaving McNabb with no offensive help. It's easy to get hyperbolic about such things, but McNabb took a team to an 11-5 record with Darnell Autry starting at running back and Torrance Small as its No. 1 wide receiver. He had no help.

Dawkins was overshadowed individually that season by McNabb's second-place MVP finish and breakout seasons for teammates Vincent and Trotter, but the Eagles went from 22nd in scoring defense in 1999 to fourth in 2000 as Johnson's defensive system took hold.

"At that point, we didn't think Jim Johnson liked any of us as players," Reese said. "Jim was a very demanding coach. He didn't tolerate mistakes and missed assignments, and he was on us from the time that meetings started until we got out to the practice field to the games on Sundays. It was good for us, because even though we were talented, we still didn't know how to win football games. We still didn't know how to have an impact on football games."

The next year, the Eagles made it to the NFC Championship Game, while Dawkins made his first All-Pro team and recorded his first playoff interception, one of four picks thrown by Tampa Bay's Brad Johnson in the Eagles' 31-9 first round victory.

Brian Dawkins *(Old man gnar at en.wikipedia)*

In 2002, Dawkins and the Eagles won the division again, and Dawkins had one of his finest seasons: 66 tackles, five forced fumbles, four fumble recoveries, three sacks, and two interceptions. The Eagles finished second in the NFL in scoring defense, allowing only 15.1 points per game, and for the first of two times in Dawkins's career, sent three defensive backs to the Pro Bowl: Dawkins and cornerbacks Troy Vincent and Bobby Taylor. Dawkins also had perhaps the best day of his career on September 29 against the expansion Houston Texans: he recorded a sack, an interception, and a forced fumble, and in the third quarter, caught a 57-yard touchdown pass from Brian Mitchell on a fake punt. No other player in NFL history has ever recorded a sack, a forced fumble, an interception, and a touchdown reception in the same game.

The 2003 season was less satisfying, as Dawkins missed nine games with a Lisfranc injury of his own, and while he was able to return for the playoffs, the Eagles suffered their third consecutive NFC Championship Game defeat.

Dawkins returned to his All-Pro form in 2004 and the Eagles, after a massive roster overhaul, went 13-3, their best season under Reid. Reid replaced three quarters of his aging secondary, replacing Vincent, Taylor, and strong safety Blaine Bishop and promoting safety Michael Lewis and cornerbacks Lito Sheppard and Sheldon Brown from within. Sheppard, Lewis, Brown, and running back Brian Westbrook were the Eagles' first four picks in the 2002 NFL Draft, a run of draft success unparalleled in franchise history.

Dawkins' new partners stepped in without a hitch: Lewis and Sheppard, as well as Dawkins, made the Pro Bowl—the second time in three years the Eagles sent three defensive backs to Hawaii. The Eagles finished second in scoring defense again, and for the first time since McNabb and Reid came to Philadelphia, had a reliable No. 1 receiver in Terrell Owens, who caught 14 touchdown passes.

The Eagles rolled through the NFC playoffs before losing by three points to New England in Dawkins's hometown of Jacksonville, Florida.

A public feud between Owens and management, and a season-ending injury to McNabb prevented the Eagles from returning to the playoffs the next year, though Dawkins returned to the Pro Bowl with a career-high 3.5 sacks, three interceptions, 70 tackles, four forced fumbles, and a career-high 24 passes defended. In 2006, at age 33, Dawkins set a new career-high with 76 tackles, forced five more fumbles and four more interceptions, and led the Eagles back to the playoffs, where they faced the New York Giants on January 7 and Dawkins made the most iconic play of his Eagles career.

It didn't change the course of the game, though the Eagles wound up winning, nor did it prevent a big play, because it resulted in a first down and the clock stopping on what would become a game-tying fourth-quarter drive for the Giants. Eli Manning found receiver Tim Carter undefended in the flat, and as Carter was racing for the sideline, Dawkins came flying in from outside the frame, legs together and arms outstretched like a person imitating a bear—literally flying, it looked like—to tackle Carter and push him out of bounds.

It was a hilarious moment, an ordinary play made special by extraordinary effort and emblazoned into the memories of Eagles fans by the menacing sight of Dawkins, his visor giving him the appearance of an eyeless monster, leaping at Carter like a cat jumping from the floor to the top of a bookcase.

In 2008, the Eagles started out 5-5-1 before sneaking into the playoffs with a 4-1 finish, punctuated by a 44-6 win over the Cowboys in Week 17 to seal a playoff berth. (This is the game that was played during the dance competition in the movie *Silver Linings Playbook*.)

As the No. 6 seed, the Eagles cruised past the Vikings and Giants in the first two rounds before trailing 24-6 at halftime in the next game against the Arizona Cardinals in the NFC Championship game. During the second half, however, the Eagles came back. McNabb took the ball with 10 minutes to go in the third quarter and led the Eagles on three touchdown drives in 14 minutes to put the Eagles up 25-24. Dawkins made four tackles in the fourth quarter alone, but the Cardinals came back to score the winning touchdown with just under three minutes left, handing the Eagles their fourth conference championship loss in eight years. Dawkins became the 10th player in NFL history to record 20 career sacks and 20 career interceptions and made the Pro Bowl in 2008, but he'd never return to the playoffs and never again put on an Eagles uniform.

That offseason was one of the most significant in franchise history. The Eagles not only released Dawkins, but Johnson, who had been diagnosed with melanoma, retired over the summer and died on July 28, 2009. After the 2009 season, McNabb, Westbrook, and Brown left the team, ending the would-be dynasty of the early 2000s and closing the book on the best years of the Andy Reid era.

Dawkins signed with the Denver Broncos before the 2009 season, and enjoyed some success there: he set a new career-high with 95 tackles, and as the Eagles' defense foundered in Johnson's absence, the calls for Dawkins to return to Philadelphia were based less in emotional attachment than they were in genuine concern for the well-being of the team. Dawkins played three seasons total in Denver, making two more Pro Bowls, before signing a one-day contract with the Eagles to retire in April 2012.

"There have been great, great players who came through Philadelphia and meant so much to the city, but I don't know if anybody connected to the fans in this city the way Brian Dawkins has," said Eagles owner Jeffrey Lurie on the day of Dawkins's retirement announcement.

On September 30, 2012, the Eagles retired Dawkins's No. 20, making him the first member of the 2000s team to be so honored, and Dawkins returned to stand by McNabb when his number was retired the following year.

The image of Dawkins thrashing around on the field, shouting at the sky, and dancing around fallen Cowboys and Giants, is somewhat incongruous with what Dawkins has become since his retirement. At his retirement ceremony, Dawkins made a point to say that he was pleased to be retiring while he still felt physically capable, that 16 years in the NFL hadn't been so hard on his body that he'd be unable to enjoy life going forward with his wife and children.

Today, Dawkins works as an NFL analyst for ESPN. He's taken off his signature armor, helmet, and visor, and given up leaping, running, and shouting in exchange for a quiet life, wearing a suit to work and discussing football calmly and candidly on TV. You almost wouldn't recognize him.

But all superheroes need a mild-mannered alter ego.

ALLEN IVERSON

17 There is no way to be clinical, objective, or detached about Allen Iverson. With him, it's personal.

So you see, there are four kinds of Philadelphia sports fan: first, the kind who love Iverson, like me, and if you love Iverson, it's because of personal subjective feelings that are very much like mine. Second, there is the kind who don't know enough about him to form an opinion, and if that's you, my reading off his stat lines and retelling his greatest moments won't adequately capture him. The third kind hates him, and nothing I write will change that. The fourth kind doesn't like basketball anyway and has probably already moved on to the chapter on Bobby Clarke.

As a sportswriter, I'm a storyteller first and foremost. I learned to write with colorful figurative language, and it's what I enjoy reading and what I do best. But when I make an argument—say, "Who are the 20 greatest athletes in Philadelphia sports history?" I'm an empiricist. I have favorites and biases and agendas, and I don't make an effort to hide them, but I try to account for those biases when I'm called on to be objective.

And the objective facts are this: Allen Iverson was a volume scorer, a chucker who led the league in scoring because of his insane usage rate. Off the court, the impact and depravity of his legal and personal problems were exaggerated by a terrified, largely white and middle class media whose cultural norms were under threat. But trouble with substance abuse, gambling, and guns has followed Iverson for 20 years, and while if you put all the Iverson stories next to the Kobe Bryant stories and Michael Jordan stories, I don't know who comes off worst, his personal history sends me scrambling for euphemisms.

I accept all of that. Iverson's not a personal hero or role model of mine, even though all the cool kids at school wore his sneakers. But everyone who loves sports, no matter how analytical, has at least one athlete for whom he has to override logic, for whom you look at the facts and say "To hell with this."

Everybody has at least one, and Iverson is mine.

Here's why. There's a feeling you get during a particularly intense moment in a particularly intense hockey game—say a line brawl in a playoff game between the Flyers and Penguins, when you think the referees are screwing your team and giving an unfair advantage to a team you not only detest personally, but also find morally reprehensible. And your team not only comes out ahead on the scoresheet, but prevails with some sort of physical violence as well. In this feeling are three separate emotional leaps: 1) The line between fan and team is blurred to nonexistence—you don't merely support the team, you *are* the team, and the team's pain is your team 2) That generates a sense of moral righteousness, which is validated in victory and 3) The good guys just simply literally beat the bad guys to a bloody pulp, which isn't righteous necessarily, but it feels good.

This feeling is a mix of blood-run-cold rage, the high of the fight-or-flight adrenaline rush, and the euphoria of joy, all mixed into one emotion that lasts only as long as Claude Giroux beats up Sidney Crosby, usually for a few seconds, maybe a minute or two.

Watching Allen Iverson was like distilling the chemical formula for that emotion, putting it in a saline solution, and having it pumped into your veins through an IV, every time you turned on the Sixers, for 10 years. Watching Iverson was intoxicating.

We talk a lot about the "Philadelphia kind of athlete," and it's almost always utter nonsense. But the Philadelphia sports mentality, such as it is, is about overcoming an inferiority complex, and doing it through an impenetrable fog of anger. That's what Iverson did—it's how he was naturally, and when he came to Philadelphia, he leaned into it. He understood it and played off it, and the fans loved him for it.

"It's going to be like that forever," Iverson said. "I am Philly."

My signature Iverson moment came in Game 1 of the 2001 NBA Finals, at the end of a two-month marathon in which Iverson overcame insurmountable odds with effortless style, it seemed, twice a week.

The thing you have to understand about the 2001 Lakers was that Shaquille O'Neal was completely unguardable.

Around the turn of the century, Shaq was in his "battleship" period—he was so big, so strong, so quick, that it was all Dikembe Mutombo, one of the greatest defensive bigs of his generation, could do to keep up with him and not foul Shaq every time he touched the ball. Then there was Kobe Bryant, also in his prime, and one of the better supporting casts of the era: Rick Fox, Robert Horry, Derek Fisher, Horace Grant, and Brian Shaw. The Sixers had Mutombo, who was hanging on to Shaq's belt for dear life, Iverson, a couple competent rotation players, and not a whole lot else.

And Iverson looked at the overwhelming odds against him and his team, bared his teeth, and ran straight into danger in a sort of berserker rage.

Midway through Game 1, NBC showed a brief highlight package indicating how the Lakers had prepared for Iverson. Backup point guard Tyronn Lue played the role of Iverson on the scout team, even going so far as to wear Iverson's signature sleeve in practice. Watching that made me angry, as if the Lakers were so arrogant to think they could duplicate Iverson, and when Lue came into the game to guard Iverson, Lue clutched and grabbed at every opportunity. The moral outrage rose until Iverson got Lue to bite on a fake baseline drive, then stepped back and hit an open long jumper. Lue leapt out to challenge the shot, but was too late, and after he landed, he tripped and fell at Iverson's feet.

That was enough, breaking free from a dirty defender with an exquisite feat of skill and athleticism. That was the act of a great athlete. But on his way back to the defensive end, Iverson took an exaggerated step over Lue's fallen body, dancing on his grave. That was the act of Iverson.

Iverson earned every bit of his anger. He grew up in Hampton, Virginia, and lived a childhood so difficult it's hard for most of the people who would go on to buy his sneakers and jerseys to understand. As a boy, Iverson grew up in a broken home and was cared for by various friends and relatives in a part of the city that was rife with drugs, violence, and poverty. Iverson himself was steered largely out of trouble by coaches and mentors who wanted to keep him from throwing away his promising athletic career, and for a while, they were successful.

Despite his lack of size—the line about Iverson was always that the size he was listed as in the media guide, six feet and 165 pounds, was exaggerated—Iverson blossomed into a state champion guard on the basketball court and a state champion quarterback and defensive back on the gridiron. But on Valentine's Day, 1993, Iverson was involved in a fight at a bowling alley that led to his arrest and, as he was already a high-profile athlete in a city divided not only among racial lines, but along lines of high school allegiance as well, Iverson's trial turned into a media circus and a referendum on race relations in southeastern Virginia. (*Hoop Dreams* director and Hampton native Steve James made an excellent 30 for 30 documentary called *No Crossover: The Trial of Allen Iverson*, which looks at the trial and its effects and should be required viewing for Iverson fans.)

Iverson served four months of a 15-year sentence before being granted clemency by Virginia governor Douglas Wilder. The conviction was overturned in 1995, by which time Iverson had left Hampton behind and gone to play for legendary coach John Thompson at Georgetown.

At Georgetown, Iverson was really good—in two seasons, he averaged 23 points and 3.2 steals per game, was twice named the Big East's defensive player of the year, and brought home first-team All-America honors as a sophomore. He then became the first person to leave Thompson's Georgetown early for the NBA.

"When I was coming out, I'll never forget when I told Coach Thompson that I was thinking about leaving, he was like 'What do you mean, you're thinking about leaving? You've got a Mercedes-Benz outside your room—I already know that. But if you need to take care of your family, take care of your family.' And he supported it. At the time I had an agent, David Falk, and I'm thinking that I'm the best player in the country," Iverson said.

That belief was validated when the Sixers made him the first pick in a 1996 draft that will go down as one of the best in league history as Iverson went in front of Bryant, Steve Nash, Ray Allen, and a handful of future All-Stars. Iverson became Iverson immediately, averaging 40 minutes a game as a rookie, leading the team in assists, steals, and points, and walking away with the Rookie of the Year trophy.

Along the way, Iverson famously crossed Michael Jordan over—and we talk about crossing people over like it's something normal, but this play involved the Sixers clearing out for Iverson against the best player in NBA history, an all-time great perimeter defender who towered over A.I. by six inches, and Iverson just destroyed Jordan, absolutely dropped his jock. That play was part of the beginning of a unique relationship.

"I honestly think it was the first season," Iverson said. "I think once I started to get the message from Larry Brown as far as how to play basketball, I got so much better once I started to look at his blueprint and play his way. And obviously my play went from just a good player to an MVP. As time goes by, you get that confidence, you have so much confidence in yourself— it's not arrogant or cocky or anything like that, you just look at yourself in the mirror and say: 'Damn, I'm the best player in the world.' And Philly fans felt like that about me too."

Brown was hired to coach the Sixers in Iverson's second season, and the two developed a close, but sometimes adversarial player-coach relationship. Iverson carried the entire offensive and entertainment burden of Brown's more conservative, defensive-minded teams, but his tendency to shoot his mouth off and his casual relationship with punctuality and, famously, practice, sometimes got him in trouble.

Iverson gets killed for the "Practice" rant, which, in terms of great moments in American oratory, is somewhere between Kennedy's "We choose to go to the moon" speech and Bill Pullman's speech before the final battle in *Independence Day*. The "Practice" rant turned one of the best athletes this city has ever seen into a punchline, but like just about everything Iverson did, it was so incredibly cool. Iverson's game alone was transcendent. Nobody that small should be able to get that high off the ground that quickly without a helicopter or something. Nobody should be able to change direction that quickly, be able to read an opponent's pass, or capitalize on a lapse in concentration as well as Iverson did. Iverson, one of the smallest everyday players in the league, led the NBA in minutes played twice and minutes per game seven times. Iverson was an average shooter, but while he could create his own long-range shot on the order of what, say, Stephen Curry does now, Iverson was nowhere near as proficient at making those shots.

So Iverson worked inside a lot, ducking and dodging men a foot taller than him who weighed twice as much, bouncing off hostile elbows and hipchecks to work for layups, or jumping passing lanes and lazy dribbles to set up scoring chances in transition. Iverson won four scoring titles not just because of his quickness, vision, and mutant handle, but also because he was tougher and worked harder than everyone else.

The best thing about it was that unlike modern athletes, who seem corporate even when they're colorful, Iverson took full advantage of his basketball skill and unparalleled self-confidence to not give a good goddamn about what anyone thought of him. Iverson's game was defined by Dizzy Dean's famous aphorism: "It ain't bragging if you can do it." And this made him the most compelling athlete I've ever seen.

Sure, we want our athletes to live right and show up to practice and not yell at the referees, but that Iverson was flawed made the least human Philadelphia athlete of the past 30 years seem like one of the most human, and therefore, relatable personalities. When we were angry, he was angry and we saw it. When he did something great, we marveled and he exulted, either shouting or cupping his hand to his ear to ask for more noise. When we were upset, he was even more upset. That's what made him so special: I'd call Iverson the basketball player the most exciting athlete I've ever seen. Add that he was a mirror for the emotions of the fans who revered him and the result is, well, here's how Iverson himself described it at his jersey retirement ceremony: "When you think about Philadelphia or athletes in general, their fan connection is nothing like the way fans connected with me in Philadelphia. It's like no other."

Allen Iverson *(Kevin Burkett)*

Iverson's other legacy was cultural. Until Iverson came along, basketball was an orderly, conservative game. It was often played with pizzazz and bravado, and Magic Johnson, Walt Frazier, Michael Jordan, and Dr. J were cool and culturally relevant, but in a nonthreatening, corporate way. Jordan hawked Big Macs and extoled familiar values while remaining carefully and conspicuously noncontroversial. Iverson wore cornrows, baggy shorts, and do-rags, festooned his body with tattoos, and didn't shy away from the hardcore hip-hop, inner-city, aggressively black culture in which he was raised, a culture that terrified many white fans. Iverson was a conspicuous individual in a sports culture that demanded conformity, and he was the first player of his generation that wasn't broken, to some extent, by that expectation. Instead, Iverson created his own expectations.

"What I'm proud of the most is changing the whole culture, changing the NBA," Iverson said. "I took a beating for it, how I look, the way I dressed, the people I hung around with, however I acted. But I enabled this generation now and took the beating so they can express themselves and be who they are."

That's what made the anger and swagger with which he played as off-putting to some as it was compelling to others. In his own way, Iverson was one of the most culturally significant figures in NBA history, like a mirror-universe Jordan.

The apotheosis of Iverson was the 2001 playoffs, which not only capped off his best season, with a scoring title and an MVP award, but was the closest he came to a title. In 22 playoff games that year, Iverson scored 50 points in a game twice, 40 points six times, and 30 points 14 times.

But there were individual moments that stand out: during the conference semifinals, he and Vince Carter conducted one of those series-long one-on-one duels that only seems possible in basketball.

Iverson dropped 54 points on the Raptors in Game 2, a franchise playoff record he'd go on to break two years later. Carter came back with 50 the next game in Toronto. When the series returned to Philadelphia tied for Game 5, Iverson collected the MVP trophy before the game, then went to work on the Raptors.

"The year I got the MVP we had a playoff game that night," Iverson said. "And the energy in the arena made me faster. It made me stronger. It made me focus even harder. It gave me so much confidence."

And it worked, because Iverson scored 52 points and added seven assists, giving him a hand in 28 of the Sixers' 47 field goals that night.

The next round, the Sixers went to Milwaukee up 3-2, but early in the first quarter, Iverson took a forearm to the throat from Bucks forward Scott Williams, and while Iverson stayed in the game, the Bucks dominated the first half, going in at halftime with a 29-point lead. By that point the game was pretty much over, but Iverson exploded for a 26-point fourth quarter and helped the Sixers cut the final margin to 10.

The next game was more comfortable. Iverson went for 44 points, and the Sixers clinched their first conference title since 1983 with a 17-point win. Iverson is the only player in the past 20 years to score 40 or more points in three straight playoff games, and only Iverson, Michael Jordan, Bernard King, Jerry West, and Kareem Abdul-Jabbar have done it in the past 50 years.

The third game in that streak, of course, was Game 1 of the Finals against the implacable Lakers. I was in eighth grade, and my grandmother had come up to watch my brothers and me while my parents were away. This was a good thing, because there was no way my parents, two very straightlaced people who didn't care a great deal for basketball or Allen Iverson, would've let me stay up until the end of an overtime game on the West Coast that seemed (at the time) to end at about one in the morning.

But Grandma let me stay up to watch Matt Geiger's 14-minute cameo, Iverson's stepover of Lue, his 52 minutes played, 41 field goal attempts, and 48 points, 30 of which came in the first half, bringing his total to 100 in the previous seven quarters. I got to see the Sixers get blown out of the water to start, just as everyone predicted, then turn a 21-8 first-quarter deficit into a 24-23 second-quarter lead.

I saw an excruciating last two minutes of the fourth quarter in which the last bucket was scored with 1:38 left on the clock. Mutombo missed two free throws as part of a 37-second possession in which the Sixers had three chances to retake the lead but didn't.

But Iverson showed up again to win the game with seven points in the last two minutes of overtime, and I don't know if basketball has ever been that good again. The next four games (all losses), might as well have not happened. And the same goes for his war with Sixers ownership, the trade to Denver in 2006, and the sad denouement to his career that eventually took him all the way to Turkey. What happened up to Game 1 of the 2001 NBA Finals was perfection.

That's what made Iverson so great: his personality, his emotion, his capacity to do things that make you wonder. Getting tied up in sports fandom is kind of an objectively silly thing for an adult to do, to have your mood determined by men you don't know playing a child's game, but Iverson validated that feeling the way no other athlete has. Only a crazy person would show as much outward emotion about anything, much less his job, as Iverson did.

For those reasons: his charisma, his skill, and the role he played in my development as a basketball fan, I've internalized something he exuded when he played. There's one set of rules for Allen Iverson and another for everyone else.

BOBBY CLARKE

18 Let's leave the question of greatness alone for a moment and talk about influence. The most influential figure in Philadelphia sports history is probably Ed Snider, the only owner in the history of the Flyers, longtime owner of the Sixers, and chairman of Comcast Spectacor—Snider was instrumental in bringing hockey to Philadelphia and constructing the Wells Fargo Center and Comcast SportsNet.

But after Snider, I don't know that anyone had a greater impact and influence, particularly as regard on-field (or on-court or on-ice) matters, more than Bobby Clarke. Despite the fact that he only stood five-foot-10 and cut his signature curly mop top ages ago, Clarke casts an immense shadow over the history of the Flyers.

Clarke was born August 13, 1949, in Flin Flon, Manitoba, where he became a junior hockey superstar with the Flin Flon Bombers of the MJHL and later WCJHL. As a seventeen-year-old, Clarke set league records with 183 points in only 45 games, then followed that effort up with 168 points in 1967–68 and 137 points in 1968–69. Despite his gaudy numbers, Clarke lasted until the second round of the NHL draft because of concerns about his health.

Clarke had been diagnosed with diabetes as a child, and while we weren't exactly using leeches and witch doctors in 1969, modern medicine's come a long way since then. There were no insulin pumps, no digital blood sugar monitors, and no real track record of diabetics playing professional sports.

"At one time, the idea of a player with diabetes playing in the NHL was ridiculous—there was no way you could do that," said Jeff Marek of Rogers Sports Net.

After passing on Clarke once, and having to be convinced by specialists at the Mayo Clinic that Clarke could hold up in the NHL with proper diet and care, Flyers GM Bud Poile picked him 17th overall in the 1969 draft.

Clarke's status as one of the first high-profile diabetic athletes made him an inspiration to young athletes with diabetes to this day: Max Domi, son of NHL tough guy Tie Domi and a Phoenix Coyotes draft pick, is himself diabetic and wears No. 16 in honor of Clarke.

Clarke needed no time to adjust to the NHL game. Without any time in the minors, Clarke played every game for the Flyers as a twenty-year-old rookie and led the team in assists.

While the Flyers were still pretty terrible when Clarke was first called up, both he and his team improved rapidly. Clarke scored 63 points in 1970–71 and got his first Hart Trophy votes. In 1971–72, he scored 81 points and won the Bill Masterton Trophy for sportsmanship and dedication.

By managing his diabetes, Clarke proved his dedication, but that summer, his sportsmanship would be tested. Clarke was selected for Team Canada in the 1972 Summit Series against the USSR, an eight-game series against the USSR that Canada won in come-from-behind fashion, an event that holds similar cultural significance in Canada that the Miracle on Ice does in the United States.

Clarke scored six points in eight games and played on a line with Paul Henderson, who scored the series-winning goal, but his most notable contribution was a slash that broke the ankle of Soviet star Valeri Kharlamov in Game 6. Clarke returned to North America a star and was named captain of the Flyers at age 23.

In 1972–73, the Broad Street Bullies started to come together with an identity that mirrored Clarke's reputation for a combination of skill and physical, mean, dirty play.

"Bobby Clarke," Marek said, "really was the quintessential Philadelphia Flyer . . . the great leader, the captain, the guy that said, 'Get on my shoulders, we're going to win this thing.' And had a vicious streak the likes of which hadn't really been seen."

Clarke took a leap in 1972–73, scoring 104 points and winning the first of three Hart Trophies. Second-year coach Fred Shero orchestrated a leap from fifth in the division to second, and brought rookie forward Bill Barber into the fold. Barber and Clarke thrived together in Shero's Soviet-inspired system.

"A lot of it relied on smart hockey players," Marek said. "And Bobby Clarke, for as much as we make of him being thuggish and dirty, he was a really smart hockey player, and so was Barber."

Barber, who scored 64 points that season, saw early on what put Clarke on a different level.

"His competitiveness, no question about it," Barber said. "His determination and his work ethic, everything that it takes to be a great player. And he worked. He worked harder than anyone else, he competed, didn't like to lose, and everything leads up to the career he had and the recognition he gets to this day."

Bobby Clarke *(AP Photo/RBK)*

The Flyers won the first playoff series in franchise history that year, dumping the Minnesota North Stars out in five games before capitulating in the next round to Montreal. Clarke led the Flyers with eight points in eleven playoff games.

The following season, Bernie Parent returned to the Flyers and helped shore up a porous defense. The Flyers went from 11th in the NHL in fewest goals allowed to first, won their second division title, and cemented their reputation as the Broad Street Bullies in advance of a historic playoff run. Clarke led the league in shorthanded goals and logged a career-high 113 penalty minutes en route to becoming, in addition to one of the league's biggest stars, one of the league's best agitators.

"I don't know that we have anyone in the game right now who's like Bobby Clarke," Marek said in Spring 2014. "I think the closest we ever had to Bobby Clarke was Mark Messier in that, one, he was highly skilled and elite among his peers, playing one of the most crucial positions on the ice, and that's center. But also, he played dirty."

Clarke, in addition to his work ethic, instilled in his teammates a pathological hatred of losing that bled over into its physical play.

"None of us liked to lose," Barber said, "and we would play accordingly at all costs to win hockey games, and we got rewarded for it."

That reward was the 1974 Stanley Cup, which the Flyers won in six games over the Boston Bruins of Phil Esposito, Bobby Orr, and Derek Sanderson. Philadelphia, instead of trying to keep the puck away from Orr, attacked him, dumping the puck into his corner, forechecking and hitting him hard to force turnovers. The next season, Clarke registered a staggering 89 assists, 125 more PIMs, and took home his second Hart Trophy en route to a Flyers repeat. That year, Clarke was reunited with his junior teammate Reggie Leach, who came together with Barber and Clarke to form the legendary LCB line. That year, Dave Schultz set an NHL record with 472 penalty minutes, while Andre "Moose" Dupont put up 276 of his own. Those totals and the on-edge play of Clarke and others made the identity of the Broad Street Bullies into something that could be stamped into history with an incident that took place on January 11, 1976.

That day, the Flyers played an exhibition game against CSKA Moscow, the Soviet Red Army team, and defenseman Ed Van Impe laid out Kharlamov (who must seem like a pitiable figure by now) with a body check so forceful, CSKA coach Konstantin Loktev pulled his team off the ice.

That reputation remains with the Flyers forty years later, though it masks, to a certain extent, how good those teams actually were.

"It's an easy story," Marek said. "I think it's really lazy, to be honest with you. Yeah, you look at Dave Schultz and Don Saleski and all those guys, Moose [Dupont] and Ed Van Impe, and it's pretty easy to say they were a pack of hounds who punched their way to the Stanley Cup . . . I think history's done that Flyers team a big disservice."

Barber laughs off the Flyers' reputation as talentless goons.

"I kind of get a chuckle out of it in the sense that we were still known as the Broad Street Bullies," Barber said. "And the thing about it was that we might have had a rough team, but we had a lot of talent on the team: guys that could score goals, make plays, play defense, win faceoffs: everything that it takes to win the championship."

In the 1976 playoffs, the Flyers were coming off their best season, with Barber scoring 50 goals and Leach scoring 61 en route to the most goals in the league and the third-fewest goals allowed, despite being without Parent for most of the season. Clarke himself turned in another 89 assists and took home another Hart Trophy.

Despite the Canadiens having finished with the league's top goal differential, the league's top scorer, Guy Lafleur, and Vezina Trophy-winning goaltender Ken Dryden, the Flyers had had some success against the Habs, coming back with five wins and three ties from their previous ten regular-season meetings.

"The reason the Montreal Canadiens had a tough time with the Flyers wasn't because of toughness," Marek said. "The Canadiens were as tough as anyone in the NHL—Larry Robinson was the Zdeno Chara of his time. The reason the Canadiens had so much trouble with the Philadelphia Flyers…was they played a Soviet style of hockey, which is damn hard to play against."

Robinson and his confreres got over it, taking down the Flyers in four straight.

The 1975–76 season would be the last in which Clarke reached the 100-point plateau. The next year, he finished second in Hart Trophy voting with 90 points, six of them on shorthanded goals, which led the league. By this point, Clarke's game was starting to evolve as he approached 30. He was still a world-class playmaker and persistent pest, but he began to shift into a more defensive role and emerge as a Selke Trophy candidate.

The second half of the 1970s was a transitional time for Clarke and the Flyers as Shero and Parent left the organization and new blood was brought in. In 1979, the Flyers' most iconic captain relinquished the captaincy to take on a new role as a player-assistant coach to Pat Quinn. Mel Bridgman took over the C as part of a new post-Broad Street Bullies generation gained traction in the organization. Clarke's final appearance in the Stanley Cup Final came in a six-game loss to the New York Islanders in 1980. Clarke was fifth on that team in points and scored 20 points in 19 playoff games.

Clarke delivered one last hurrah in 1982–83, scoring 85 points, his highest total since 1977–78, and as a 34-year-old, took home the Selke Trophy as the league's top defensive forward. Clarke played one more year and posted 60 more points before calling it quits for good in 1984.

Here's the record Clarke left behind: three Hart Trophies—all other Flyers in history have combined to win one. He holds the Flyers' single-season record for assists. Clarke is the Flyers' all-time leader in assists, games played, points, plus / minus, and shorthanded goals. Clarke is also fourth in franchise history in goals and fourth in penalty minutes. He captained the only two championship teams in franchise history, and of the five other conference championship teams the Flyers have ever iced, Clarke played on and coached one and constructed three more as general manager.

Speaking of general managers, Clarke, who had been president of the NHLPA during his playing career, switched sides and joined management. Clarke ascended to the Flyers'

GM position immediately after he retired and got to work immediately, putting the finishing touches on a team of young players who had mostly been drafted by Bob McCammon, and the Flyers went to the Stanley Cup Final in 1985 and 1987 under Mike Keenan, a first-time NHL head coach Clarke had hired after McCammon's resignation.

Clarke was fired by the Flyers in 1990, after which point he landed on his feet as general manager of the Minnesota North Stars. Clarke's time as GM of the North Stars was eventful: on November 22, 1990, he traded goalie Kari Takko for defenseman Bruce Bell, a transaction that warmed the hearts of Mexican food fans across the nation who will forever remember the "Takko-Bell trade." He also gave Bob Gainey his first NHL head coaching job, and despite finishing 27-39-14, the North Stars, led by Brian Bellows, a young Mike Modano, and Clarke's former teammate Brian Propp, made a surprising run to the Stanley Cup Final in 1991. Clarke left Minnesota for warmer climates after the 1992 season, spent a year as senior vice president of the Flyers, then left again to become GM of the expansion Florida Panthers. (The North Stars would do the same, moving to Dallas in 1993.)

Clarke constructed the Panthers' original roster, claiming former Flyers Scott Mellanby and Gord Murphy in the expansion draft and building around future Flyer goalie John Vanbiesbrouck. Clarke lasted a year in Florida before returning to Philadelphia to replace Russ Farwell.

Farwell was the man behind the Eric Lindros trade and had failed to reach the playoffs in four seasons.

Clarke's second stint as Flyers GM lasted 12 seasons and was fraught with ironies: first, after having won two Stanley Cups as a player with the best goalie in the world behind him, the one piece Clarke never got as a GM was a top-notch goalie. Even the two Vezina winners from his first stint with the Flyers, Pelle Lindbergh and Ron Hextall, were McCammon draftees. Clarke famously passed on free agent goalies Mike Richter and Curtis Joseph in the summer of 1998 to sign an aging Vanbiesbrouck, and despite having some of the best forwards in the game under his watch, Clarke made only one Stanley Cup Final in his second stint with the Flyers.

The second is that while Clarke wasn't actually the GM who traded for Eric Lindros, his feud with Lindros and Lindros's parents would come to dominate the memory of his time as Flyers GM. (In the interest of not devoting two chapters of this book to Clarke v. Lindros, you should see the Eric Lindros chapter for a more thorough discussion.)

After trading Lindros in 2001, Clarke tried to paper over the Flyers' faults with a series of high-priced veteran signings, but the Flyers were perennial second-round or third-round victims, and once the NHL opened up the game and instituted a salary cap after the 2004–05 lockout, Clarke found himself increasingly behind the times. His final season, 2005–06, was a first-round playoff exit that set up a disastrous 2006–07 season during which his successor, Paul Holmgren, pretty much rebuilt the team from scratch.

Nevertheless, just as Clarke, in his first go-around as Flyers GM, benefited from Bob McCammon's draft picks,

Clarke didn't leave the cupboard bare for Holmgren: he drafted Simon Gagne, Jeff Carter, Mike Richards, Joni Pitkanen (who would be traded for Joffrey Lupul, who would, in turn, be the centerpiece of the package that brought back Chris Pronger in 2009), and Claude Giroux.

After drafting Giroux in 2006, Clarke stepped down as GM on October 22, returning to his role as senior vice president on December 4 of that year, a position in which he remains today.

As I write, Clarke is sixty-four years old, and he's spent 42 of those years, in some position or other, as a member of the Flyers' organization. To some extent, he remains the face of the organization. He is absolutely the franchise's defining driver of team identity and its all-time greatest player.

MIKE SCHMIDT

19 Mike Schmidt would make any city's list of 20 greatest athletes. He was certainly adequately appreciated when he played, but like so many of baseball's best two-way players, might actually have been slightly underrated when he played.

By any objective standard, Schmidt is the best third baseman ever to play the game. Among third basemen since 1901, Schmidt is first in home runs, eighth in OBP (maybe seventh if David Wright declines at all before he's done), and second in slugging percentage, .002 behind Chipper Jones. Schmidt accumulated 106.5 WAR in his career (60 is usually a good benchmark for the Hall of Fame), 10 more than second-place Eddie Mathews.

Schmidt ranks ninth all-time among right-handed hitters in career home runs, though Albert Pujols will pass him. Which is not to say Pujols is the only right-handed hitter who will ever pass Schmidt—Giancarlo Stanton or Mike Trout or someone else will probably get there eventually. But of the eight right-handed hitters with more home runs than Schmidt, only Alex Rodriguez didn't play first base or outfield.

Which speaks to something that gets lost about Schmidt, who is often viewed as a great power hitter and nothing else. First of all, being a great power hitter at a position other than first base and outfield is a pretty rare thing, particularly when the power hitter in question was as good a defender as Schmidt. Schmidt won 10 Gold Gloves over the course of his career, which doesn't say as much about his defense as it should, because the Gold Glove is a defensive award that usually goes to a good hitter rather than the best fielder. A better way to state Schmidt's defensive ability is that he's eighth all-time in defensive WAR among third basemen. That's not a perfect measure, particularly considering that advanced defensive metrics from the 1970s and 1980s are reverse-engineered from existing data, but Schmidt, the great power hitter, is somewhat behind Adrian Beltre, Scott Rolen, and Clete Boyer, but not by much.

Among Phillies players, Schmidt is first in home runs and games played and second in hits, after Jimmy Rollins passed him in June 2014. His .380 OBP is fifth among Phillies players with at least 3,000 plate appearances with the team since integration and his .527 slugging percentage is third. That WAR total is, as of April 2014, more than Jimmy Rollins's and Chase Utley's WAR total put together.

Schmidt lapped the field in terms of both peak and consistency. In 1974, Schmidt posted a 9.7 WAR season, the best season by a Phillies player since integration. (For reference, you'd expect two to three wins from an average player, about five from an All-Star, and eight from an MVP candidate.

A 10-win season will usually get a book, or at least a *Sports Illustrated* cover story, written about it.)

That 1974 season started a string of 14 consecutive seasons of 5 WAR or more for Schmidt, who was worth seven or more wins in nine of those seasons. Ryan Howard's career high is 5.2 WAR—Schmidt tied or beat that total 13 times in his career. Rollins' career high is 6.1—Schmidt tied or beat that 13 times as well.

Mike Schmidt was ridiculously good.

Mike Schmidt was born September 27, 1949 in Dayton, Ohio, and he stayed close to home for college, attending Ohio University in Athens, where he was a star shortstop. My favorite fact about Schmidt has to do with his draft position. In 1971, the Phillies chose him in the second round, one spot behind George Brett.

Bill James, who also has a soft spot for that piece of trivia, called Schmidt and Brett the two best third basemen ever. I don't know if I'd agree with that, but I wouldn't argue with anyone who puts Brett, Wade Boggs, or Chipper Jones second behind Schmidt.

Anyway, Schmidt's path from twenty-one-year-old draftee in 1971 to twenty-four-year-old superstar in 1974 was neither particularly long nor convoluted, but it was kind of weird.

The overwhelming majority of major league position players played catcher, shortstop, or center field either up until the moment they were drafted or signed, or close to it. That's because most major leaguers were the best players on their high school or college teams, and if you played Little

League, you know that the best players played up the middle.

Anyone who's not among the very elite moves to a less challenging position over time, either because of innate ability or because of the propensity of young men to get bigger and slower as they age.

Schmidt was pretty typical in this regard—like most high draftees, he was a shortstop in college, and like most six-foot-two shortstops with 500-home run power, he moved to third base when he reached the big leagues. However, Schmidt played relatively little of third base until he reached the majors—79 minor league games at short, 76 at second base, fifty-nine at third.

Schmidt rose very quickly through the minor leagues: in only his second pro season, 1972, he spent the entire season at AAA Eugene in the Pacific Coast League with future World Series teammates Bob Boone and John Vukovich, as well as outfielder Oscar Gamble, who is famous for having the most outrageous afro in baseball history.

Schmidt killed AAA as a twenty-two-year-old. He hit 26 home runs in 531 plate appearances and cranked out a .291/.409/.550 line, for which the Phillies felt compelled to reward him with a late-season call-up.

The 1972 Phillies were terrible. This was the team, you might remember, that won only 59 games despite Steve Carlton winning 27. Schmidt made his major league debut on September 12, taking over for Don Money in the second inning of a 4-3 loss to the Mets before being replaced himself by Larry Bowa in the ninth. Schmidt went 1-for-3 with a walk. By this point, Schmidt had moved almost exclusively to third base—he'd play 157 games at first base and 24 at shortstop through the rest of his career.

After a 13-game cameo, Schmidt took over third base in April 1973 after Money was traded. So far, there's nothing unusual about the story—it's not unusual for prospects, particularly college draftees who hit as well as Schmidt did, to go from draft to starting lineup in less than 24 months.

What is unusual is that Schmidt was godawful in 1973. As a twenty-three-year-old rookie, Schmidt hit .196 in 443 plate appearances and struck out 136 times. That's pretty ugly, but the Phillies were the sixth-place team in 1973, so what did they care?

The good news is that the foundation for Schmidt's bounce-back in 1974 were laid. Despite his unsightly batting average, Schmidt led the team in walks and posted a .324 OBP. He also hit 18 home runs, stole eight bases in 10 attempts, and had a decent year with the glove. These secondary skills that were the difference between washing out completely as a rookie and earning a second chance also put Schmidt over the top once he learned to put bat to ball.

Which he did with a vengeance in the next year: .282/.395/.549, 23 stolen bases and a league-leading 36 home runs, the first of eight times he'd lead the National League in home runs. Though his 138 strikeouts also led the National League, Schmidt compensated by doing more when he made contact—in 1974, Schmidt had 71 extra-base hits, whereas the year before, he'd had only 72 hits of any kind.

And that's just the kind of player Schmidt was for the next

14 years—at least 30 home runs, elite defense, close to 100 walks.

Mike Schmidt *(AP Photo)*

Meanwhile, the Phillies were getting better too, and Schmidt got more recognition as the 1970s wore on. He made the All-Star team for the first time in 1974, and would do so in 12 of the next 16 seasons. In 1976, the Phillies won 101 games, their highest win total ever, and outscored their opponents by more than 200 runs en route to their first playoff berth since 1950.

Along the way, Schmidt had one of the more memorable games of his big league career. The Phillies have a habit of playing bizarre games against the Chicago Cubs, and their game on April 17, 1976, is only secondarily notable because the Phillies overcame two different 10-run deficits.

In his later years, Harry Kalas was fond of ruminating about days at Wrigley Field where the wind was blowing out, and this game was one of them. Steve Carlton, en route to a fourth-place Cy Young finish, got absolutely shelled for seven runs in 1 ⅔ innings, and the Phillies found themselves down 12-1 after three innings and down 13-2 after four.

Schmidt had had a rough start to the season, dropping from third to sixth in the Phillies' lineup after only a week. After the game, Schmidt told the *Philadelphia Inquirer*'s Allen Lewis that "Really, deep down you don't think [we had a chance]. But maybe the lack of pressure helped. You just go up there and work on your swing. I needed a game like this to take off some of the pressure."

With that pressure off, Schmidt hit four home runs in his last four at-bats, driving in eight runs to spark a remarkable comeback. The Phillies scored two in the fifth inning, three in the seventh, five in the eighth, and three more in the ninth to take a 15-13 lead, which Tug McGraw blew.

"Smitty never would have done it without me," McGraw joked.

In the top of the 10th inning, having homered in the fifth, seventh, and eighth innings, Schmidt took Paul Reuschel out for two runs and the eventual winning margin, tying the record for home runs in a game. Schmidt's 1976 went pretty well after that. Schmidt scored his first Gold Glove and his first top-3 MVP finish and appeared in the postseason for the first time. While Schmidt went 4-for-13 with two doubles in the NLCS, the Phillies were swept out of the playoffs by the Cincinnati Reds.

The next season Schmidt was slightly better and the Phillies returned to the playoffs, this time scoring their first playoff win in 62 years in Game 1 of the NLCS. It was Schmidt's ninth-inning RBI single off Elias Sosa that put the Phillies up for good. Two games later, the Phillies broke a 3-3 tie with two eighth-inning runs off Sosa for a chance to go up 2-1 in the series. If the Phillies had held on to Game 3, they'd have sent Steve Carlton to the mound, at the Vet, for a chance to go to the World Series. Bill Coniln of the *Daily News* described the crowd as "on their feet, a shrieking chorus that all afternoon had roared with the blood lust of a Roman Coliseum mob rooting for the lion."

Three outs from victory, the Phillies bungled away that chance. Greg Luzinski, who would have ordinarily been replaced by Jerry Martin for defense, misplayed a fly ball in a Buckneresque moment that didn't exactly do wonders for manager Danny Ozark's job security. The next play, Davey Lopes lined a one-hopper that deflected off Schmidt to Bowa, whose throw appeared to beat Lopes to first base, but umpire Bruce Froemming called him safe. The Phillies went on to melt down in an episode that went on to be known as Black Friday.

Conlin's description of the crowd after the 6-5 loss: "In a collective silence reserved for the demise of a great matador in a jammed Plaza de Toros."

A powerful image, and difficult to overcome, though Schmidt and the Phillies eventually did in 1980.

At age thirty, Schmidt won his first MVP. He hit .286/.380/.624, played 150 games of stellar third base defense, and hit 48 home runs, a career high and, at the time, the second-highest total ever for a third baseman. Carlton won his third Cy Young that year, and the two led the Phillies to 92 wins, past the Astros in a nerve-racking NLCS and to a World Series showdown with Brett and the Kansas City Royals.

In the World Series, Schmidt went completely berserk. He hit .386/.462/.714 with two home runs in six games. Schmidt homered in the Game 5 win and drove in the series-winning run with a third-inning single in Game 6 to take home World Series MVP honors.

The next season, Schmidt successfully defended his MVP season with probably the best year of his career: .316/.435/.644, all career highs, with 31 home runs and 7.7 WAR, which is MVP-worthy in a regular season, but good enough to disturb the fabric of the universe in a strike-shortened season in which Schmidt played only 102 games. There's no guarantee Schmidt's numbers would have extrapolated out over a full season—the midseason break might have helped the 31-year-old Schmidt recover, but if he'd played 153 games at the same rate, he'd have put up an 11.5 WAR season.

Considering that most modern ballplayers start declining in their 30s, what Schmidt did on the back half of his career was pretty insane: he led the National League in OPS+ six times in seven seasons after turning thirty and posted more WAR after age 30 than his teammate and fellow Hall of Fame third baseman Tony Perez did in his entire career.

After an NLDS loss in 1981 and a World Series loss in 1983, Schmidt never played in the playoffs again, and the increasingly aging Phillies team jettisoned much of its core from 1980: Rose, McGraw, Carlton, Boone, and replaced them by 1986 with younger faces: Steve Bedrosian, Darren Daulton, and Juan Samuel. Schmidt was the constant, and in 1986, at age thirty-six, he won his third and final MVP, which, at the time, tied the record.

Schmidt played 160 games and led the league in home runs, slugging percentage, intentional walks and OPS+ for the last time.

Schmidt made the All-Star team again in 1987, but in 1988, he missed the last third of the season with injuries and suffered his worst season since his disastrous rookie campaign. Dissatisfied with his play on his return in early 1989, Schmidt retired suddenly on May 25, though he was coaxed out of retirement to play in one last All-Star game.

On Schmidt's retirement, Jayson Stark, then a young writer for the *Inquirer* who would go on to a celebrated career of his own, wrote that Schmidt's enduring legacy would be as a player who made the game look easier than it was:

> He may have fired those home runs off into the night, but he never shook the earth trying to launch them.
>
> He never went tumbling to one knee like Reggie. He never glowered like Frank Robinson or towered like Willie McCovey.
>
> They just came flowing out of him—so smooth, so easy, so natural. Dick Allen hit lightning bolts. Greg Luzinski hit moon shots. Mike Schmidt just hit baseballs that wouldn't come down.
>
> And how will you describe the way a 10-time Gold Glove-winner played third base? With many of those same words: *smooth, easy, natural.*
>
> He wasn't much for flopping around in the dirt, making a lot of plays that looked more spectacular than

they were. That wasn't Mike Schmidt's style.

His style was to make the spectacular plays look *easier* than they were, not the other way around. And that was a trick only the great ones could turn.

The Phillies retired his number a year and a day after Schmidt himself retired, May 26, 1990. Four years later, in his first year of eligibility, Schmidt was inducted to the Hall of Fame with 96.5 percent of the vote.

Unlike many other Philadelphia legends, who stepped away from playing the game only to commit the second half of their lives to broadcasting, coaching, or management, Schmidt has largely taken his retirement seriously, golfing, fishing, and only dabbling in media and coaching. In the mid-2000s, Schmidt toyed with returning to the game full-time, managing the Phillies' A-ball affiliate, the Clearwater Threshers, in 2004, and serving as an assistant coach on Team USA in the 2009 World Baseball Classic. Schmidt is currently working part-time as a color commentator on Phillies broadcasts, but unlike Bob Clarke, Tom Gola, or Richie Ashburn, there isn't really a second act for Schmidt's career.

The enduring image of Schmidt is therefore still as a player—stance closed, sideburns and mustache groomed like a highway cop in a 1970s TV show, ready to come out of his shoes to swing at a hanging breaking ball.

The image is of the best third baseman ever, the best Phillies player ever, and one of the greatest athletes in Philadelphia sports history.

WILT CHAMBERLAIN

20 The holy grail of the sports hypothetical is the time machine. The inability to accurately and definitively determine how athletes would do in different eras makes it very difficult to compare athletes over the course of history.

The good news is that we have a workaround to one very particular time machine question: what would happen if you took a modern center, a mobile, athletic seven-foot-one, 275 pounder with good hands and multi-sport training, and dropped him in the early 1960s, an era where Bob Pettit, a six-foot-nine bald white guy who operated entirely below the rim, could average 25 and 15 every year for 12 years as one of the dominant bigs in the NBA?

We have the answer because Wilt Chamberlain, a center with 1990s skills, 1990s size, and 1990s athleticism, descended on the NBA in 1959 as if he'd been sent from another galaxy to harvest Earth's natural reserves of points and rebounds as revenge for the destruction of his homeworld.

In actuality, Wilt Chamberlain was born August 21, 1936 in Philadelphia, across town from the arena where he'd turn into the best player of his era. By the time he arrived at Overbrook

High School in Philadelphia, Chamberlain had already grown to six-foot-11, and if his size and athleticism overwhelmed NBA opponents, you can imagine what he did to high schoolers. There are very, very few major league athletes who were so good that the league had to change the rules to stop them, so you can imagine how unprepared the high school game was for a player like Chamberlain. Chamberlain once scored 60 points in 12 minutes, and Overbrook's coaches sometimes instructed other players to miss free throws intentionally so Chamberlain could put them back for two points. In three varsity seasons, Chamberlain lost only three games and scored 2,206 points despite facing opponents who, in the absence of a shot clock, would often try to hold the ball to keep it away from Chamberlain and Overbrook.

In 1955, he went to college, opting to attend the University of Kansas instead of staying close to home. Barred from playing varsity as a freshman, Chamberlain led the JV team to a victory over the Jayhawks' varsity in a scrimmage, and as a sophomore, Chamberlain was inserted into the starting lineup immediately.

In 1956–57, the Jayhawks found themselves without the services of legendary head coach Phog Allen. Allen had coached the Jayhawks' basketball team for a total of 39 seasons in two stints, between which he went to medical school, and originally took over the job in 1907 from James Naismith, who invented basketball. Allen had won both a national championship and an Olympic gold medal in 1952 as a head coach, and could count both Adolph Rupp and Dean Smith as his students.

Allen turned the program over to lead assistant Dick Harp in 1956, Chamberlain's first year on varsity. They didn't suffer much, as Harp and Chamberlain took Kansas to within a point of another national title. After the 1957–58 season, Chamberlain decided to leave school, but NBA rules prevented him from joining the league until after his class had graduated, so Chamberlain spent a year with the Harlem Globetrotters instead.

When Chamberlain was draft-eligible the next year, it took some chicanery to get him on the Warriors. At the time, NBA rules allowed a team to use its first-round pick to select a local college player, regardless of draft order. The Warriors had used this rule to great effect in the years previous, selecting Tom Gola out of La Salle and Paul Arizin out of Villanova. Though Arizin and Gola were both Philadelphia natives as well, that was incidental. As commonly understood to that point, territorial draft rules applied only to local college players, not players like Chamberlain, who had gone to high school in an NBA city but played their college ball elsewhere. Nevertheless, Warriors owner Ernie Gottlieb convinced the league to give Chamberlain to the Warriors, where he was inserted into the starting lineup alongside Gola and Arizin. His impact was immediate and profound.

Chamberlain tied for the league lead in minutes played as a rookie, led the league in scoring and rebounding, and was named the league's MVP, becoming the first of two players in league history to win Rookie of the Year and MVP honors in the same season. Chamberlain pulled down more rebounds than any three of his teammates put together, scored 2,707 points (Gola and Arizin together scored 2,728) and made the second-most free throws in the league despite shooting only 58.2 percent from the line. That season, Chamberlain met his longtime rival, Bill Russell, in the playoffs for the first time, and the two teams set up the script they'd follow for the next decade: Chamberlain would outplay Russell on the offensive end, but thanks to superior coaching by Red Auerbach and a superior supporting cast, the Celtics would blunt Chamberlain's impact enough to come out on top.

This seems as good a time as any to debunk the bizarrely pervasive myth that Russell was a better player than Chamberlain. Any pro-Russell argument is grounded in two things: 1) He was the best defensive center of his generation, if not of all time and 2) His Celtics teams routinely beat Wilt's Warriors and Sixers teams in the playoffs.

I'd rebut those claims by saying 1) Yes he was and 2) Yes, they did. However, there's never been a better offensive player or rebounder, relative to his competition, than Wilt. I bring this up now because in 1961–62, Wilt averaged 50.4 points, 25.7 rebounds, and 48.5 minutes per game, and remember, a regulation NBA game is only 48 minutes long. And yet Russell was named the league's MVP over Chamberlain. Russell and Chamberlain were roughly equivalent per-game rebounders over their careers (Chamberlain pulled down 22.9 boards per game, while Russell had 22.5 in slightly fewer minutes). Without block or steal numbers, much less advanced metrics and SportVu cameras, it's tough to say for sure how good a defender either Russell or Chamberlain was, but in this 1961–62 season, the Celtics had the best defense in the league on both a per-possession and per-game basis, while the Warriors allowed the most points per game, but thanks to playing at the league's highest pace, ranked third in per-possession defense. And insofar as we can reverse-engineer win shares, Russell led the league in defensive win shares in 1961–62. However, three of the next four players on the list were Russell's Boston teammates, and the only non-Celtic to break the top five was Chamberlain, who came in second.

In a league where, again, Bob Pettit could pull down 18.7 rebounds per game, Chamberlain must've been a plus defender because his size allowed him to protect the rim and pull down more rebounds than anyone else.

So Russell's a better defender, and I'll even stipulate that his edge on defense was non-trivial.

Yet arguably the most important difference lies in their scoring ability. In 1961–62, Wilt scored 4,029 points. Second place went to Walt Bellamy, who scored 2,495. Russell also recorded a career-high points total in 1961–62, with 1,436. Put Russell's points total together with that of the second-place scorer, and you still wouldn't have matched Wilt's total.

This would be less of a big deal if his gap over Russell weren't so enormous, and also if scoring points weren't the object of basketball. Sure, Wilt took 3,159 field goal attempts that season, but I'd rather have him making 50.6 percent of those shots than give them to the Warriors' second-leading scorer, Paul Arizin, who shot 41 percent from the floor. Russell was the third option on a relatively egalitarian Celtics team that had five players take 1,000 or more shots, resulting in the seventh-worst per-possession offense in a nine-team league.

Chamberlain played almost every minute of every game and almost literally lapped the field in terms of quantity of offensive production while maintaining an elite level of efficiency as well. Russell's edge on defense, while considerable, doesn't come close to matching Chamberlain's edge on offense. Put in numerical terms, Russell's career defensive win shares dwarf Chamberlain's: 133.6 to 93.9. Russell is first all-time, Chamberlain fifth. On offense, Chamberlain beats Russell 153.3 to 29.9. Chamberlain's total is second behind Kareem Abdul-Jabbar's, and in a neighborhood with Michael Jordan and Oscar Robertson. Russell is 293rd all-time, having just missed out on being a better offensive player, relative to his competition, than Sleepy Floyd.

The common retort is that Russell won 11 NBA titles to Chamberlain's two. And that counts for something. But saying that distorts the truth: the Celtics won 11 titles, while the Sixers and Lakers won one each. Russell and Chamberlain weren't the only players on the floor, and holding up team success, without context, as a measure of individual achievement is facile and reductive. Great players tend to play on great teams, but they don't *always* play on great teams for their entire careers: some supporting casts are so underwhelming not even a talent such as Chamberlain could elevate them above Russell—himself one of the greatest basketball players ever—and a superior band of sidekicks.

It also presupposes that playoff success matters to the exclusion of regular-season achievement and that there's an easy translation from team playoff success to individual moral fortitude. (Because that's how these debates are always framed, as if Chamberlain's failure to win more titles is a failure of character more than it is a failure of not being drafted by the team run by Red Auerbach. By the way, no modern pro sports executive was ever more ahead of his competition than Auerbach, with the possible exception of Branch Rickey.)

In the playoffs, Russell averaged 16.2 points and 24.9 rebounds per game on 43 percent shooting from the field and 60.3 percent shooting from the line for a PER of 19.4 and .178 win shares per 48 minutes. Chamberlain averaged 22.5 ppg and 24.5 rpg on 52.2 percent shooting from the field and 46.5 percent shooting from the line for a 22.7 PER and .200 WS/48.

That Russell-led Celtics teams beat Chamberlain-led Warriors, Sixers, and Lakers teams seven times out of eight despite Chamberlain having moderately better career playoff numbers than Russell is a pretty powerful argument for how great the Celtics of the 1960s were. It is not, however, compelling evidence that Russell was the superior player. Maybe Russell did have some innate metaphysical ability to affect the outcome of important games, a "clutchness," as some people like to call it. However, I'm more inclined to believe that Russell, while a stupendous player and monumental historical figure in his own right, wasn't quite as good as Chamberlain, rather than believe that he possessed abilities that escape the statistical (i.e. factual) historical record.

It's far easier to believe that Russell's Celtics were better-put together and better-coached, and that in a short series, anything is possible—even in eight short playoff series. Barring some new information, any attempt to say that Russell was a better player than Chamberlain is an attempt to talk around an obvious empirical truth.

Wilt Chamberlain

(Fred Palumbo, World Telegram staff photographer)

But enough about Bill Russell.

You don't get to 50.4 points per game without an outlier or two. The most famous outlier came on March 2, 1962, when Chamberlain scored 100 points a game, which is still by far the highest total ever, in a game against the New York Knicks. A little more on his scoring prowess: Not only does Chamberlain hold the single-game and single-season scoring records, his

50.4 points per game in 1961–62 is more impressive in the following context. The next season, he averaged 44.8 points per game. Nobody else has ever broken 40 ppg for a season, and of the nine seasons in which an NBA player averaged 35 points per game, Chamberlain is responsible for five.

The next season, the Warriors picked up and left for San Francisco, and Chamberlain's supporting cast was further diluted with the departure of its other two local heroes. Arizin retired rather than move west, and an aging Tom Gola found himself getting homesick and asked to be traded back East. The Warriors accommodated him after 21 games with a trade to the Knicks.

Chamberlain once again led the league in scoring, rebounding, minutes and PER, but the newly-minted San Francisco Warriors, relieved of Arizin and Gola, dropped to 31-49. Midway through the next season, Chamberlain himself was shipped back East, returning to the city of his birth and the Philadelphia 76ers. The .500 team suffered another seven-game defeat to the Celtics, this time losing in the closing moments on the famous "Havlicek stole the ball!" play.

As Chamberlain entered his late twenties and suddenly found himself with his best secondary scoring option (Hal Greer, the Sixers' all-time leading scorer) and his best complementary big man (Billy Cunningham, who was drafted fifth overall out of North Carolina in 1965), he began to shoulder much less of the offensive load.

In 1965–66, Chamberlain won his seventh scoring title in his seventh NBA season, but he'd never win another. He did, however, lead the NBA in rebounding every year until he retired, except for 1969–70, when a knee injury limited him to twelve games.

After another division final loss to Boston in 1966, Chamberlain found himself in a different role the next season under new head coach Alex Hannum. With Greer, Cunningham, and Chet Walker around to shoulder some of the scoring load, Chamberlain stepped back and delivered a season that was as impressive in its efficiency as 1961–62 had been in its volume. Despite leading the team in minutes, Chamberlain turned from scorer to playmaker as the Sixers ran an inside-out offense in which Chamberlain still led the team in scoring, but took what was then a career-low 1,150 field goal attempts, tied for third on the team. Instead, Chamberlain accounted for more assists than any two of his teammates combined, 630 in total, and the Sixers married their third-ranked defense to the NBA's top offense, starting 45-4 before finishing with a then-NBA record 68 wins. Chamberlain also shot 68.3 percent from the field, which set a new single-season record for players with at least 1,000 attempts. In the nearly 50 years since, nobody's even come close to breaking it. Kevin McHale, Kareem Abdul-Jabbar, and Shaquille O'Neal, three of the best offensive big men who followed Wilt, have each barely squeaked over the 60 percent mark once.

In the playoffs, Chamberlain made and won his first NBA Finals as the Sixers knocked off the hated Celtics in a five-game division final, then took out Chamberlain's former team, the Warriors, in six games to win it all.

In 1967–68, Chamberlain became the first and only big man to lead the league in total assists, with 702, though Oscar Robertson had more assists per game. Chamberlain nevertheless won his fourth MVP (and third in a row), and the Sixers once again posted the league's best record at 62-20. Once again, Russell and the Celtics awaited in the Eastern Division Finals. (Though with Russell approaching his mid-30s, saying "Havlicek and the Celtics" would probably be more accurate.)

In 1968, the Celtics came back from being down 3-1 to win the series, with Chamberlain's last game in a Sixers uniform coming in a 100-96 Game 7 defeat in which he pulled down 34 rebounds but didn't shoot the ball in the second half.

That offseason, Hannum jumped to the Oakland Oaks of the ABA, and Chamberlain, upset at Hannum's departure and in search of a bigger stage, requested a trade. Sixers GM Dr. Jack Ramsay sent the four-time MVP to the Los Angeles Lakers for Jerry Chambers, Archie Clark, and Darrall Imhoff, whom Chamberlain had once torched for 100 points when Imhoff was a member of the New York Knicks.

In each of his three NBA stops, Chamberlain's two primary supporting players were Hall of Famers, and he seemed to upgrade each time he got traded, from Gola and Arizin to Greer and Cunningham and finally to Jerry West and Elgin Baylor in Los Angeles.

Chamberlain's move to Los Angeles was in many ways the beginning of the end. It might not have looked like it at the time, because Chamberlain could drop 20 and 20 as easily as you or I might take out the garbage, but age and, for the first time, injury, began to slow the Big Dipper down. Chamberlain arrived in Los Angeles and immediately found himself as the third scoring option behind Baylor and West, and for the first time in his career, Chamberlain did not lead his team in scoring in 1968–69. He still scored 20.5 ppg, led the league in rebounds, and shot 58.3 percent from the floor, however, as the Lakers won the Western Division regular season and playoff titles.

In 1969, Chamberlain found his path to the finals blocked by Russell's Celtics for the last time, and sure enough, the Celtics scored another playoff victory, this one a 4-1 win in the NBA Finals.

The next season, Chamberlain's knee limited him to twelve regular-season games, making 1969–70 the only season of his career in which Chamberlain didn't make the All-Star team. He returned to lead the Lakers in minutes in the playoffs, but in Game 7 of the NBA Finals, Chamberlain found himself on the wrong end of another famous moment in playoff history: Knicks center Willis Reed, suffering from an injury to his thigh muscle, returned to score the first four points of the game and, as the legend goes, inspired his team to the upset victory. Chamberlain won another rebounding title in 1970–71, but the Lakers again lost in the playoffs, this time to the Milwaukee Bucks.

Nine games into the 1971–72 season, Baylor retired, and immediately after, the Lakers won 33 games in a row, still a record in North American professional sports, and cakewalked to the title. The 1971–72 Lakers won 69 games, breaking the record set by Chamberlain's Sixers five years before, and won 12 of 15 playoff games behind the league's top offense, keyed not only by West and Chamberlain, but also by wings Jim McMillan and Gail Goodrich.

By 1972–73, Chamberlain was thirty-six years old, and while he still led the team in minutes and the league in rebounds, he was no longer the reliable volume scorer he'd been in his youth. Chamberlain took a career-low 586 shots, sixth on the team, though he finished second to West in assists and shot an astonishing 72.7 percent from the floor. That off-season, Chamberlain jumped to the San Diego Conquistadors of the ABA to be their player-coach, but the Lakers, who held one more year of Chamberlain's contract, filed an injunction that prevented him from playing.

Chamberlain coached the Conquistadors, who were led by future Sixers center Caldwell Jones, to a 37-47 record and a 4-2 loss in the conference semifinals to Utah. Chamberlain never played or coached in professional basketball again.

In his later years, Chamberlain was involved in various business ventures and flirted with rumored comeback attempts that didn't subside until the 1980s. A multi-sport star in his youth, Chamberlain opened a successful track and field club and hired Bobby Kersee to coach it. Then a college coach, Kersee would go on to become one of the most successful sprint coaches in history. Chamberlain also dabbled in professional volleyball and acting, notoriously landing a part in *Conan the Barbarian* in 1984. (While the Wilt-Kareem argument continues on the court, Kareem Abdul-Jabbar's role in *Airplane* proved Chamberlain's successor as Lakers center to be the superior actor.)

Though he remained fit throughout his retirement, Chamberlain battled heart issues late in life and died on October 12, 1999 at the age of sixty-three.

Chamberlain left behind a legacy of offensive dominance so great, so impossible to believe that it's discounted, I think, as much out of disbelief as it was out of anyone else having claim to being the best player of the 1960s. Because I believe the quality of play has improved over time, I wouldn't call Chamberlain the best player of all time—I'd put him behind Michael Jordan, LeBron James, Shaq, Kareem, and maybe a few others. But nobody in the history of North American team sports stood out over his competition the way Chamberlain has. He was the greatest player in the history of both of Philadelphia's NBA franchises and the best player on the best basketball team in the city's history. Relative to his competition, he's the greatest team sport athlete to be born in Philadelphia or its suburbs.

For those reasons, Wilt Chamberlain is the greatest athlete in Philadelphia sports history, and calling him that isn't a particularly difficult choice.

EPILOGUE

Not only is any ranking of great athletes at least somewhat subjective, but it's also fluid. So just for fun, how could this list have looked different, and how might it look different ten or twenty years from now?

Well, for starters, it's not a slam dunk that Tom Gola was the best Philadelphia college product to go on to play for the Warriors in the 1950s—Paul Arizin could have ended up in his spot. In fact, if anything, basketball is underrepresented on this list: if Bernie Parent is on this list thanks to only a few great years that led the Flyers to a title, how much worse is Moses Malone's case? For that matter, the Sixers' all-time leading scorer, Hal Greer, didn't make the cut, but could have. If you value longevity over peak value, you might rather have Brian Propp represent the 1980s Flyers on this list rather than Ron Hextall. Somewhere between Charles Barkley and Donovan McNabb, the list goes from sure-thing all-time greats, no-doubt Hall of Famers who left an indelible mark on the city's history to outer-circle Hall of Famers with lesser credentials. At any rate, that's where it gets hazy.

As of the summer of 2014, Jimmy Rollins is enjoying something of a career renaissance, playing his best baseball in three years at age thirty-five while laying siege to the franchise lea-derboard in all sorts of counting stats. If he plays well through 2015, it'll be hard to make the case for Ashburn over Rollins. Then there's Bobby Abreu, who didn't play in Philadelphia as long as Rollins, and was even less popular when he did. But look at the numbers: Abreu was durable and good at pretty much every aspect of the game, and on a rate basis, better than any player in franchise history except Schmidt and Utley.

But that's all in the past. Let's look to the future: who could make it onto the next iteration of this list?

As it happens, Philadelphia sports isn't exactly awash in would-be Hall of Famers at the moment, but even barring something unexpected, like the Phillies trading for Mike Trout or Nerlens Noel unexpectedly becoming the best defensive center in NBA history, there are a couple names.

First, Flyers center Claude Giroux, twenty-six, is already one of the best playmakers and two-way forwards in the league, a Hart Trophy finalist, and a point-per-game playoff scorer. He's got a long way to go, obviously, because we might have said the same thing about Mike Richards and Jeff Carter when they were Giroux's age, and we know how that turned out. Look a little farther down the line and Sean Couturier could have a Bill Barber-type career, but that's getting a little ahead of things.

Things are a little clearer in baseball: in the near future, Utley can move up the list and Rollins could sneak onto it, but Cole Hamels is the real contender if he stays healthy and effective through the end of his current contract. He's already, as of May 2014, fourth in franchise history in strikeouts, tied for third in ERA+, fifth in WAR, and first in K/BB ratio, at age 30. Between now and 2019, he could wind up right there with Carlton.

Among current Eagles, LeSean McCoy stands to rack up stats as the center of a fast-paced, run-heavy offense, though the lifespan of an NFL running back being what it is, nothing is certain in the long term. Finally, Le Toux, at age thirty, still has a long way to go in his career, but defenders Sheanon Williams and Amobi Okugo are both younger and equally entrenched in the Union's long-term plans, insofar as any MLS team has long-term plans. Okugo in particular is only twenty-three, already in a leadership role with the Union, and as a longtime fixture in the U.S. national youth setup, could make an impact on the international level that wasn't available to Le Toux. I'd bet on Okugo being on this list in 20 years before any other soccer player.

Of course, all of this is speculation and all of this is unpredictable. The debate will go on, and we'll know about the future when it comes.

INDEX